Ram Niwas Lakhotia is one of India's top authorities on taxation and practices as an advocate and tax consultant, specialising in practical tax planning and the drafting of trusts and wills.

Starting with a brilliant academic career – Mr Lakhotia was ranked first in both his graduate and post graduate examinations in Commerce – he joined the Indian Revenue Service as an Income Tax Officer, Class I. He again stood first in the whole country in the Income Tax Officers' Examination. Later, he quit the revenue service and launched into a highly successful taxation practice.

Spreading the message of tax planning far and wide, Mr Lakhotia has addressed thousands of lecture meetings, symposia, and seminars on tax planning. He has written dozens of books on income tax, which have run to over 490 editions. He has been interviewed over BBC, London, A.I.R., Hong Kong Radio, Zee News TV, Star News TV and Doordarshan. Every Sunday at 8.30 P.M. as "Tax Doctor" he answers questions of viewers over Zee Business TV Channel. He was conferred an Honorary Degree of Doctor of Taxation by Giani Zail Singh, a former President of India. He is the Founder-President of Income Taxpayers Association and Rajasthani Academy, and the Principal of Lakhotia College of Taxation and Management. He is the President of Vegetarian Congress of Delhi and Veg 4 you.

Interested in the spread of practical spirituality and vegetarianism, he has written books on the subject of life improvement, and edits a monthly journal, *Excellent Living.* In the field of social service, he has constructed a big *Dharamshala* (rest house) for the use by families of the patients of JLN Hospital, Ajmer. He has served as the District Governor of Lions Clubs International, and was awarded the prestigious *Udyog Rattan Award, Samaj Gaurav Award, Samaj Ratna Award, Manav Seva Puraskar, Distinguished Personality Award, Torch-Bearer of Vegetarianism Award and Lal Bahadur Shastri National Award.*

TAX PLANNING
for NRIs

(Assessment Year 2008-2009)

R. N. Lakhotia

VISION BOOKS

(Incorporating Orient Paperbacks)

New Delhi • Mumbai • Hyderabad

www.visionbooksindia.com

Third Edition 1993
17th Edition 2007

ISBN 10: 81-7094-703-0
ISBN 13: 978-81-7094-703-5

© R.N. Lakhotia, 2007

Published by
Vision Books Pvt. Ltd.
(Incorporating Orient Paperbacks & CARING imprints)
24 Feroze Gandhi Road, Lajpat Nagar 3
New Delhi 110024, India.

Phone: (+91-11) 2983 6470 or 2983 6480
Fax: (+91-11) 2983 6490
E-mail: visionbk@vsnl.com

Printed at
Rashtra Rachna Printers
C-87 Ganesh Nagar, Pandav Nagar Complex,
Delhi-110091, India

Contents

Preface to the seventeenth edition

In dealing with all types of taxpayers, including non-resident Indians for over four decades, what I have found in common among most non-resident Indians is that they are grossly ignorant of the tax-saving aspects of their own income, although fortunately for them, several tax concessions have been announced under the Indian tax laws in recent years.

The present book is a practical guide to non-resident Indians in the matter of planning their residential status and enjoyment of maximum exemptions, deductions, and other tax concessions available under different Direct Tax Laws as amended by the Finance Act, 2007 together with the essential aspects of practical relevance to NRIs as per FEMA. The relevant rules and regulations under FEMA have been analysed in this edition. The book offers complete guidance to a non-resident Indian in the matter of adoption of proper tax planning so as to minimise his tax liability in India while remaining outside or on returning to India with a view to permanently residing here. This book will serve as a practical guide on tax planning for such Indians as it has been profusely illustrated with practical problems with their solutions and is written in a non-technical language so that non-resident Indians who are not very well conversed with Indian tax laws can understand these provisions and plan their investments, gifts, and income for themselves as well as the members of their family. The chapters on FEMA have enhanced the utility of the book immensely.

The book would not have been printed in time without the assiduous labour put in by my eldest son Subhash Ch. Lakhotia, Income Tax Consultant. I am also grateful to my numerous non-resident clients and friends for the various suggestions and problems posed by them from time to time, which have been incorporated in the book. I also thank Shri Kapil Malhotra for publishing this revised edition in its present form.

May, 2007
S-228, Greater Kailash - II
New Delhi - 110048
Ph. 2921 5434 and 98110 25800
E-mail: thelakhotia@gmail.com
     slakhotia@satyam.net.in

R. N. LAKHOTIA

CHAPTER 1

How to become a non-resident Indian and save income tax in India

1. Introduction

A non-resident individual in general or a non-resident Indian (NRI) in particular pays less income tax in India on his income under the provisions of the Income Tax Act, 1961, in comparison with a resident individual. Hence, wherever possible, an individual, going abroad should so plan his residential status that he is a non-resident in India in a particular year to be able to legally save the maximum amount of income tax. The expression non-resident for the purpose of income tax in India is different from the expression as used under the FEMA, *viz.*, Foreign Exchange Management Act, 1999. The meaning of the expression non-resident under the FEMA is relevant for investment of funds in India and hence the special meaning assigned to the expression non-resident Indian under that Act has been dealt with in Chapter 4. In this chapter as well as in the following chapters till Chapter 10, the expression non-resident or non-resident Indian has been used as it is understood in the Income Tax Act, 1961, which is the main enactment governing the levy and assessment of income tax in India. The expressions NRI or a person resident outside India and the special concessions for their investment in India as per FEMA have been discussed in Chapters 11 onwards.

2. Classification of individuals on the basis of residential status

The incidence of income tax payable by an individual in India varies according to his residential status. Hence, it is necessary for the correct determination of income tax liability to determine the residential status of the individual taxpayer. Individuals may have any of the three residential status under the income tax law in India:

(a) Resident but not ordinarily resident in India;
(b) Resident and ordinarily resident in India; and
(c) Non-resident.

The meaning of the expressions, "Resident but ordinarily resident", "Non-resident", and "Resident and ordinarily resident in India" have been explained in the subsequent paras.

3. Who is a non-resident?

A person who is not a resident in India in any previous year is said to be a non-resident individual. The expression "previous year" has been explained in detail in Chapter 2, topic 5.

An individual is said to be non-resident in India in any previous year (which is the financial year immediately preceding the assessment year concerned), if neither of the following two conditions applies to him:

(a) If he is in India in that year for a period or periods amounting in all to 182 days or more.
(b) If, he, within the four years preceding the relevant previous year, has been in India for a period or periods amounting in all to 365 days or more and he is in India for a period or periods amounting in all to 60 days or more in that year.

Where an individual does not fulfil either of the aforesaid two conditions, he would be classified as non-resident individual in India. Where, however, an Indian citizen leaves India in any previous year as a member of the crew of an Indian ship or for the purposes of employment outside India the period of 182 days would be substituted for 60 days in the first condition.

Likewise, where an Indian citizen who has gone abroad and comes back to India on a visit in any previous year, the period of 182 days would be substituted in place of 60 days, for the purposes of determining his residential status.

These conditions can be understood by means of a few examples given on next page.

Illustration No. 1

A, who is a citizen of India leaves India for the first time on 5 April 2007 for taking job in the U. S. A. He does not intend to come back to India for the next two years. As the total residence of A in India is for a period of 5 days only during the financial year 2007-2008 he would be said to be non-resident in India for the previous year (financial year) 2007-2008 relevant to the assessment year 2008-2009. For a detailed meaning of the expression "assessment year", please refer to Chapter 2, topic 5.

As per Section 2(30) "non-resident" means a person who is not a "resident", and for the purposes of Sections 92, 93 and 168 includes a person who is not ordinarily resident under Section 6(6).

Illustration No. 2

B has been residing in India since 1983. During the financial year 2007-2008, i.e. during the previous year (for income tax assessment purposes) from 1.4.2007 to 31.3.2008 he leaves India on 21 May 2007 to do business in London for a period of three years. During the previous year 2007-2008 the total stay of B in India was only 51 days, namely 30 days in April and 21 days in May 2007. During the last four years preceding the relevant previous year (i.e., during 2003-2004 to 2006-2007), his total stay in India has been for a total period of 365 days or more, yet as his physical stay during the previous year 2007-2008 does not amount to 60 days he would be considered to be non-resident in India.

Illustration No. 3

C left India for a job in West Germany in the year 2005. Prior to that he always remained in India. During the financial year 2007-2008 he intends to visit India during the vacations and plans to stay for 180 days. The residential status of C during the previous year 2007-2008 would be that of non-resident in India. This is because he does not physically stay in India for 182 days and, thus, the first condition is not fulfilled. Secondly, though his physical stay in India during the last four years has been for periods amounting in all to 365 days or more, yet he has not been in India for 182 days. As C has come to India on a visit, the period of his stay in India is increased from 60 days to 182 days for the second condition. As his physical stay during the previous year 2007-2008 is only 180 days, he would not be fulfilling the second condition also. Hence, he would be considered to be a non-resident individual in India.

4. Who is a Non-resident Indian?

A non-resident Indian enjoys certain extra tax concessions in comparison with an individual who is simply a non-resident, i.e., who is a foreigner. Under the provisions of Section 115C (e) of the Income Tax Act 1961, a "Non-resident Indian" means an individual, being a citizen of India or a person of Indian origin who is not a "resident". Thus, every Indian citizen who is a non-resident in India in any previous year is considered to be a non-resident Indian. Likewise, if an individual is not a citizen of India, and, is a person of Indian origin, who is non-resident in India in any particular previous year, he would also be known as a non-resident Indian. A person shall be deemed to be of Indian origin if he, or either of his parents or any of his grandparents was born in undivided India. This means that an individual who is not a citizen of India can also be considered to be a non-resident Indian, if he can prove that either his parents or any of his grandparents or parent was born in undivided India. This may be illustrated by means of an example.

Illustration No. 4

D left Lahore in the year 1945. A son, S, was born to him in Hongkong in the year 1949. S has never come to India so far. S intends to visit India during the financial year 2007-2008 relevant to the Assessment Year 2008-2009. As the father of S was born in Lahore which was a part of undivided India, he would be known as a non-resident Indian; if he is otherwise not a "resident" in India as per provisions explained in topic 3 above.

---

5. When is a person resident but not ordinarily resident in India?

An individual who is a resident in India falls into one of two classes, namely:

(i) Resident but not ordinarily resident in India; and

(ii) Resident and ordinarily resident in India or ordinarily resident.

Under the provisions of Section 6 (1) of the Income Tax Act, an individual is said to be resident in India (or simply resident in India) in any previous year, if he fulfils *any one* of the following two conditions:

(a) He is in India in that year for a period or periods amounting in all to 182 days or more.

(b) Having within the four years preceding that year he has been in India for a period or periods amounting in all 365 days or more, and he is in India for a period or periods amounting in all to 60 days or more in that year.

The period of 60 days as mentioned in the second condition is changed to 182 days in the case of an Indian citizen who leaves India in any previous year as a member of the crew of an Indian ship or for the purpose of employment outside India. Likewise, there is another situation in which the period of 60 days of the second condition is changed to 182 days in the case of an Indian citizen who, being outside India, comes on a visit to India in any previous year. The purpose of his visit is immaterial for the this condition.

These provisions may be explained by means of a few examples given below :

Illustration No. 5

E is a person of French origin. He comes to India in the month of April 2007. He is in India till the end of 2007. As the physical stay of E in India would be for a period amounting to 182 days or more, he would be considered to be resident in India during the previous year 2007-2008 relevant for the Assessment Year 2008-2009.

Illustration No. 6

F Left India for higher studies in June 2005. This was the first occasion that he left India on a visit abroad. He comes to India on 2 April 2007 to attend the marriage ceremony of his sister. He leaves India on 10 September 2007. From these facts it is clear that F has stayed in India during the four years preceding the financial year 2006-2007 for 365 days or more. Further, he has come to India on a visit from abroad during the financial year 2007-2008 and has stayed in India for 162 days (from 2 April 2007 to 10 September 2007). He would be considered a non-resident in India in the financial year 2007-2008 relevant to the Assessment Year 2008-2009.

Illustration No. 7

G leaves India for the first time on a foreign trip to do business in the U. S. A. on 1 June 2007. He does not intend to return to India for at least two years. Let us determine his residential status in India. As the physical stay of G in India during the financial year 2007-2008 is not 182 days, the first condition for making him resident in India is not fulfilled. However, he has stayed in India during the preceding four financial years, namely, 2003-2004, 2004-2005, 2005-2006 and 2006-2007 for a period amounting to 365 days or more and has also stayed in India for a period amounting to more than 60 days. He would be considered to fulfil the second condition. As G has not left India for the purpose of employment outside India, but, only for the purposes of business outside India, the period of 60 days will not be enlarged to 182 days. Thus, his status would be that of resident in India on the fulfilment of the second condition. If G were to leave India on 1 June 2007 or before for the purpose of employment outside India, then he would be considered to be non-resident in India as he would be less than 182 days in India.

The Finance Act, 2003 had, w.e.f. the A.Y. 2004-2005 made a substantial amendment of far-reaching importance adversely affecting the income-tax liability of NRIs who are interested in becoming "resident but not ordinarily resident in India". Earlier, till A.Y. 2003-2004 a person could become a "resident but not ordinarily resident in India" if he did not fulfil any of the following two conditions of Section 6(6), viz:

(a) He has been resident in India for nine out of ten previous years preceding the relevant year; or

(b) He has been in India for a period or periods, amounting in all to 730 days or more during the seven previous years preceding the relevant year.

Thus, if an individual who was non-resident, for any two consecutive previous years would, on his arrival and stay in India in the subsequent year, become and remain so as a "resident but not ordinarily resident" in India for the next 9 subsequent previous years. This would mean that he would not be liable to income tax in India on his foreign income for the next 9 years.

However, the Finance Act, 2003 has, w.e.f. the A.Y. 2004-2005, substituted Section 6(6) with the following:

6 (6): A person is said to be "not ordinarily resident" in India in any previous year if such person is —

(a) an individual who has been a non-resident in India in nine out of the ten previous years preceding that year, or has during the seven previous years preceding that year been in India for a period of, or periods amounting in all to, 729 days or less, or

(b) a Hindu undivided family whose manager has been a non-resident in India in nine out of the ten previous years preceding that year or has during the seven previous years preceding that year been in India for a period of, or periods amounting in all to 729 days or less.

Thus, a non-resident person for 9 previous years till the previous year ending on 31-3-2003 would be regarded as a "resident but not ordinarily resident" in the previous year 2003-2004 even if he is a resident in India in the Financial Year 2003-2004. But not so for the previous year 2004-05 (relevant to the A.Y. 2005-06) as the number of previous years he was a non-resident would be reduced to 8 only. However, if his total stay in India during the seven previous years ending on 31-3-2003 has been 729, or less, he would be a "resident but not ordinarily resident" in India, even if he were to return to India for good. This is explained in Illustrations No. 8 & 11.

6. When is a person resident and ordinarily resident in India?

The incidence of income tax differs to a great deal on the residential status of an individual, as has been explained in detail in Chapter 3. The maximum incidence of income tax is in the case of a person who is resident and ordinarily resident in India. The income liable to tax in the case of such an individual is much higher than what is the case for a non-resident individual. Hence it is important to know the meaning of the expression "resident and ordinarily resident". According to Section 6(6) of the Income Tax Act, 1961 an individual can be said to be "resident and ordinarily resident in India" if he is resident in India during the relevant previous year as explained in topic 3 above and does not fulfil any of the conditions for becoming not ordinarily resident in India.

An individual who fulfils the above condition will be known as an ordinary resident during the relevant previous year. Such a person is also known as "ordinary resident". The determination of the residential status as ordinary resident is explained by means of a few examples given next.

Illustration No. 8

H left India for an assignment as a Mechanical Engineer in London 8 years ago and has not visited India during the last four years. His stay in India during the seven years preceding the financial year 2007-2008 totalled 720 days. During the financial year 2007-2008, H was resident in India. It is clear that H was not a non resident in nine out of the ten previous years preceding 2007-2008. But, as his total stay during the preceding seven years amounts to 720 days, he would not be known as a resident and ordinarily resident in India. His correct status would be that of "resident but not ordinarily resident" in India.

Illustration No. 9

Mr. I (a person) went out of India for studying abroad in the year 1981. He has been visiting India from time to time. During the financial years 1997-98 to 2006-2007, i.e. the ten financial years preceding the current financial year 2007-2008, he was a non-resident in India for nine years. His total stay in India during the financial years 2000-2001 to 2006-2007, i.e., the seven years preceding the current financial year 2007-2008 was 732 days. Mr. I is also going to be a resident during the financial year 2007-2008. On these facts as Mr. I has not fulfilled the conditions laid down in Section 6 (6), he would be classified as a person who is "resident and ordinarily resident" in India for the A.Y. 2008-2009.

Illustration No. 10

J leaves India for the first time to take up an assignment abroad in the month of April 2007. He is not likely to return to India during the next three years. Even though J has been a resident in India for nine years during the last ten years preceding 2007-2008 and has also been in India for a period amounting in all to 730 days or more, he would still not be known as ordinarily resident in India. This is because he would be a non-resident in India during the financial year 2007-2008 relevant to the Assessment Year 2008-2009.

7. Precautions you should take when leaving India for the first time in order to become a non-resident

Whenever a person leaves India for taking up an employment outside India, he must leave India at such a time that during the relevant financial year his total stay in India does not become 182 days but is only 181 days or less. This precaution, if taken by an individual, can help him become non-resident in India during the

---

Illustration No. 11

K, a British national, was appointed as Senior Scientific Officer in India on 1 April 1999. He stayed in India for 700 days during the 7 years preceding the previous year. During the financial year 2007-2008, K would be a resident in India. He would not be considered as ordinary resident in India. He would be known as "resident but not ordinarily resident" in India because of his stay in India during the preceding 7 years being only 700 days.

Illustration No. 12

L intends to leave India for the first time to take up an employment in Japan, on 30 September 2007. The physical stay of L in India during the financial year 2007-2008 is for a period of 183 days (from 1 April 2007 to 30 September 2007). As this period exceeds 181 days he would be resident in India. If L had taken the precaution of leaving for employment abroad on 28 September or before, instead of 30 September, then his residential status would have been different. In that case, his total stay in India during the financial year 2007-2008 would have been only 181 days or less and he would be a non-resident in India for the financial year (or previous year) 2007-2008 relevant to the A.Y. 2008-2009.

Illustration No. 13

M leaves India to start business in the USA on 8 July 2007. Prior to this date he has always been in India. On these facts, it is clear that M does not leave India for the purpose of employment outside India. Hence, the condition of physical residence in India from 60 days to 182 days as per Section 6(1) of the Income Tax Act (see topic 5 above) does not apply to him. M has been in India for 365 days or more during the financial years 2003-2004 to 2006-2007, i.e. four previous years preceding the current financial year 2007-2008. Hence his residential status in India during the financial year 2007-2008 relevant to the Assessment Year 2008-2009 would be that of resident in India. If M were to leave India not for the purposes of business, but for the purpose of employment outside India, he would become a non-resident in India.

relevant financial year. This relaxation is applicable only to a person who leaves India for the purpose of employment outside India and not otherwise. Thus, when a person leaves India for the purpose of business or profession outside India, he can become a resident in India even if his stay in India amounts to 60 days or more during the relevant financial year, provided he has been in India for a period amounting to 365 days or more during the four years preceding the relevant financial year.

8. Precautions you should take when coming to India on leave for retaining your non-resident status

Very often Indian citizens who have gone out of India for purposes of employment outside India or for purposes of business or profession ask a common question about the duration of stay in India on a visit. During holidays etc. while visiting India, they are worried that on account of their stay they may become resident in India. Hence a non-resident normally tries to keep his actual stay in India to 181 days or less so that he is non-resident in India in the previous year. The period between the day of his arrival in India and the day of his departure from India would be considered as the period of actual stay in India, for calculation of his stay as a non-resident for 181 days or more. Thus, where an individual who has gone out of India visits India during the financial year 2007-2008 and who wishes to maintain his status as that of a non-resident in India should so plan the date of his arrival and departure, as well as the period of physical stay in India that the total period of his stay in India including the day of his arrival and day of his departure does not exceed 181 days. It may be mentioned here that this condition is applicable only for those persons whose physical stay in India has been for a period of 365 days or more during the last four previous years preceding the relevant previous year. Thus, where the total stay of a person in India is 364 days or less during the last four financial years, namely, 2003-2004 to 2006-2007 immediately preceding the relevant financial year 2007-2008 for the purpose of becoming a resident in India he must stay in India for 182 days or more. Hence, in the case of an individual who fulfils condition (b) as laid down in topic 5 above, i.e., who has a physical stay of 365 days during the last four previous years preceding the relevant financial year, must be careful to see that his stay in India is kept for 181 days only, so that he can continue to enjoy the benefit of being known as non-resident in India even for the financial year or the previous year 2007-

2008, relevant to the Assessment Year 2008-2009. This aspect may be explained by means of a few examples given below.

9. How to remain a resident, but not ordinarily resident in India, even after permanently returning to India

We have seen in para 6 above that a resident in India has to fulfil any of two conditions laid down in Section 6(6) of the Income Tax Act 1961, to become not ordinarily resident in India. Thus, where a resident in India does not fulfil the conditions, it would amount to a higher

---

Illustration No. 14

N left India to take up a job in London two years ago. Prior to that he was ordinarily residing in India. He visits India on 3 October 2007 to attend the wedding of his brother. He wishes to remain a non-resident in India during the financial year 2007-2008. He must so plan his stay and final departure from India that he leaves India latest by 31 March 2008. According to this suggestion, if he leaves India on 31 March 2008, then his total stay in India would be for 180 days only, namely 29 days in October 2007, including the day of his arrival, 30 days in November 2007, 31 days in December 2007, 31 days in January 2008, 28 days in February 2008, and 31 days in March 2008, including the day of his departure from India.

Illustration No. 15

O left India for working in Italy, about eleven years ago. He has been visiting India from time to time since then. However, his actual stay in India in any year has never exceeded 60 days. During the financial year 2007-2008 he arrives in India on 4 April 2007 and leaves India on 10 September 2007. He is worried about becoming a resident in India because his actual stay in India (from 4.4.2007 to 10.9.2007) has been for 160 days. As O has not stayed in India for at least 365 days during the financial years 2003-2004 to 2006-2007 the second condition as mentioned in topic 5 would not be applicable. Only the first condition is applicable to him for making him a resident in India. And, that condition is regarding the actual stay in India for a period of 182 days or more. As this condition is not fulfilled by him, O would be non-resident in India during the year 2007-2008 relevant to the Assessment Year 2008-2009.

incidence of Income Tax in India, particularly on his foreign income. As explained in Chapter 2, the foreign income of a resident individual is normally not liable to income tax in India even if he returns to India permanently. The foreign income is taxable in India only in the case of an ordinarily resident-person. Hence, most individuals returning to India with a view to settling for good would like to maintain the status of "resident but not ordinarily resident in India" which means the fulfilment of at least one of the two conditions laid down in Section 6(6) and explained in topic 5. It could be so planned by a person returning to India permanently that he might be a non-resident in nine years before returning to India. In such a case, the individual would continue to enjoy the status of "resident but not ordinarily resident" and would be liable to tax only on his Indian income and not on foreign income, in most cases. This is because one of the condition for making an individual not ordinarily resident individual in India, which is that he should be a non-resident in India for at least nine years in the ten years preceding the relevant financial year is fulfilled. Where this is not possible for an individual, he should be able to plan his actual stay in India in such a manner that the physical stay in India does not exceed 729 days in India during the last seven years preceding the relevant year in which he returns to India. This aspect of tax planning is explained by means of illustrations given below.

Illustration No. 16

P, who has been out of India for the last twenty years, returns to India permanently on 28 April 2007. P has income from certain investments outside India, the actual amount of which is Rs. ten lakh. He is afraid of being taxed on this income in India.

On the above facts P will not be liable to tax on the income from investments outside India for at least two years, namely 2007-2008 and 2008-2009 as he will be able to fulfil at least one condition of Section 6(6), namely being a non-resident for nine years during the ten years preceding the relevant financial year. It is only during the financial year 2009-2010 that a change in his residential status could occur.

---

10. Rules for determining the residential status of non-individuals, like a Hindu Undivided Family, a firm or an association, or a company

A Hindu undivided family, firm or any other association of persons or a body of individuals is said to be a resident in India in any previous

---

Illustration No. 17

Q has been out of India for about 25 years. He has returned to India on 15 May 2007 with a view to permanently settling in India. In the previous years 2002-2003 and 2006-2007 he was non-resident in India. However, during the previous years 2003-2004, 2004-2005 and 2005-2006 he was resident but not ordinarily resident in India.

The tax planning to be adopted by Q for remaining a resident but not ordinarily resident in India for a maximum period after his return to India would be different from the tax planning adopted by P in Illustration No. 16. As Q has been a non resident in India in the previous years 2002-2003 to 2006-2007, he would not enjoy the status of resident but not ordinarily resident for the previous years from 2007-2008. This is because during the ten previous years, namely 1997-1998 to 2006-2007, immediately preceding the previous year 2007-2008 he was a non resident in India for only five years, namely 2002-2003 to 2006-2007.

---

year in every case except where during that year the control and management of its affairs is situated wholly outside India, as per Section 6(2) of the Income Tax Act. Thus, even if part of the control and management of the affairs of a Hindu undivided family or partnership firm or any other association of persons is situated in India, it would be considered to be a resident in India. As explained in topic 5 above, as per the substituted Section 6(6) by the Finance Act, 2003, w.e.f. the A.Y. 2004-2005, a Hindu undivided family would be said to be "not ordinarily resident" in India in any previous year if its manager has been a non-resident in India in nine out of the ten previous years preceding that year, or has during the seven previous years preceding that year been in India for a period of or periods amounting in all to 729 days or less. Thus the "resident but not ordinarily resident" or "resident and ordinarily resident" status of an H.U.F. would depend only on the residential status of its manager from the A.Y. 2004-2005. A *company* as per Section 6(3) of the Income Tax Act 1961 is said to be resident in India in any previous year if :

(i) it is an Indian company ; or

(ii) during that year, the control and management of its affairs is situated wholly in India.

However, *any other person* is said to be resident in India as per Section 6(4) in any previous year in every case, except where during that year the control and management of his affairs is situated wholly outside India. Where a person is a resident in India in a previous year relevant to an assessment year in respect of any source of income he would be deemed to be a resident in India in the previous year, relevant to the assessment year in respect of his other sources of income, as well, as per Section 6(5) of Income Tax Act. As regards non-individual assessees, there is no distinction between a resident and an ordinary resident. Thus, if a firm or a company is resident in India during any previous year, it would also be considered as resident and ordinarily resident in India in that year.

11. Conclusion

As explained in the various illustrations given above, a person who is ordinarily residing abroad or who returns to India permanently could also continue to be a non-resident or a resident but not ordinarily resident in India for a limited number of years, thus making him liable to less income tax in India in comparison with an ordinary resident individual.

CHAPTER 2

Preliminary aspects of tax planning for NRIs

1. Introduction

A non-resident Indian can save a good deal of income tax in India by adopting the legally accepted methods of tax planning. Both income tax and wealth tax can be saved by a non-resident Indian if he follows tax planning in the matter of residential status as explained in the previous chapter. Likewise, the other aspects of tax planning which he has to follow for saving income tax have been described in the subsequent chapters. In this chapter we shall be dealing with the preliminary aspects of tax planning like the meaning of the expression "assessment year", "previous year", etc. and the direct tax laws which affect the non-resident Indian, and the computation of total income, etc. which affect the incidence of income tax. Therefore, it is essential for a non-resident Indian to grasp the provisions relating to other preliminary aspects of tax planning as discussed in this chapter, before embarking on the actual implementation of tax planning ideas for himself and the members of his family.

2. The direct tax laws which affect NRIs

The most important direct tax laws which affect the non-resident Indian and his investments and income in India are:

(a) *Income Tax Act 1961*. This is the main enactment which deals with the levy, assessment, and collection of income tax on residents as well as non-resident persons in India. It is supplemented by certain rules known as Income Tax Rules 1962.

(b) *Wealth Tax Act 1957*. This Act regulates the levy and collection of wealth tax of individuals, Hindu undivided families and companies in India. This is also supplemented by certain rules made under this Act which are known as Wealth Tax Rules 1957.

(c) *Gift Tax Act 1958.* This Act concerns the levy and collection of gift tax on the gifts made by donors till 30 September 1998. It allows various types of exemptions, including certain special exemptions in respect of gifts made by non-resident Indians. From 1-10-1998 there is no Gift-tax

(d) *Finance Act.* Every year the Parliament passes a Finance Bill which lays down the rates of income tax for a particular financial year, known as the assessment year. The rates of wealth tax and gift tax are contained in the respective enactments, concerning wealth tax and gift tax. Amendments to the various direct tax laws are also inserted through the Finance Act and sometimes through the Direct Tax Law Amendment Act or the Tax Amendment Act.

(e) *Board Circulars.* The Central Board of Direct Taxes, New Delhi, is the apex administrative body for the different tax laws in India. It issues circulars giving relief and granting tax concessions as also interpreting the provisions of the different direct tax laws for the guidance of the taxpayers. The circulars issued by the Central Board of Direct Taxes are known as Board Circulars and are binding on the different income tax authorities administering various direct tax laws.

(f) *Notifications.* The Government of India issues notifications and publishes them in the Official Gazette from time to time. Some of the notifications have the effect of granting special exemption from income tax to certain specific items. Sometimes, a notification lays down a particular date or amount concerning a particular tax provision or concession. Hence, it is necessary for a taxpayer to be in touch with the important notifications affecting his own facts and circumstances.

In this book we have dealt with the relevant provisions of the direct tax laws which are of particular importance for non-resident Indians in enabling them to adopt proper tax planning for saving their taxes. The new law concerning foreign exchange transactions, etc., is known as FEMA, i.e., Foreign Exchange Management Act 1999, and is not a part of direct tax laws. Hence the provisions of FEMA have not been dealt with in this chapter but in separate chapters 11 to 18.

3. Incomes of NRIs liable to income tax

Income tax is payable by a taxpayer whether a resident taxpayer or a non-resident taxpayer or a non-resident Indian on the total income computed by the Assessing Officer under the provisions of the Income

Tax Act 1961. Under Section 5(2) of the Income Tax Act a non-resident is liable to pay income tax on the total income of a particular year derived from whatever source, which:

(a) is received or is deemed to be received in India in such year by or on behalf of such persons, or

(b) accrues or arises or is deemed to accrue or arise to him in India during such year.

The Authority for Advance Rulings in the case of *Steffen, Robertson & Kirsten Consulting Engineers & Scientists* v. *CIT* (1998) 230 ITR 206 has held that where the amounts are paid for preparatory study in a foreign country to a non-resident for services which are to be utilised in India, such amounts would be deemed to accrue or arise in India. In this case, it was also held that there is no difference between fees for Engineering Services and amounts paid as living allowances and travel allowances.

Thus, only Indian income is liable to income tax in India in the case of a non-resident person. This means that a non-resident person is not liable to pay any income tax in India on his foreign income. Though an income may not actually accrue or arise in India, yet it may be deemed to accrue or arise in India. Thus, under Section 9 (reproduced below) the following are the important types of income which are deemed to accrue or arise in India:

(i) Income through any business connection in India, or through or from any property in India, or through or from any asset or source of income in India or through the transfer of a capital asset situated in India.

(ii) (a) Salary income for service rendered in India; and
(b) Salary for the rest period or leave period which is preceded and succeeded by services rendered in India and forms part of the service contract of employment from the A.Y. 2000-2001.

(iii) Salary payable by the government to a citizen of India for service outside India.

(iv) A dividend paid by an Indian company outside India.

(v) Interest by the government, etc.

(vi) Royalty payable by the government or others in some cases.

(vii) Fees for technical services payable by the government or others in some cases.

In *Asian Development Service* v. *CIT* [1999] 239 ITR 713, it was held where in respect of placement of an amount to a non-resident, tax liability was to be borne by the resident, the tax liability of non-resident was to be determined with reference to the gross figure. The Finance Act, 2003 has, w.e.f. the A.Y. 2004-2005 inserted Explanations 2 & 3 in Section 9(1) (i) as under:

Section 9 is reproduced below:

Income deemed to accrue or arise in India

9.(1)   The following incomes shall be deemed to accrue or arise in India:—

(i) all income accruing or arising, whether directly or indirectly, through or from any business connection in India, or through or from any property in India, or through or from any asset or source of income in India, or through the transfer of a capital asset situated in India.

Explanation1. For the purposes of this clause—

a)   in the case of a business of which all the operations are not carried out in India, the income of the business deemed under this clause to accrue or arise in India shall be only such part of the income as is reasonably attributable to the operations carried out in India;

(b)   in the case of a non-resident, no income shall be deemed to accrue or arise in India to him through or from operations which are confined to the purchase of goods in India for the purpose of export;

(c)   in the case of a non-resident, being a person engaged in the business of running a news agency or of publishing newspapers, magazines or journals, no income shall be deemed to accrue or arise in India to him through or from activities which are confined to the collection of news and views in India for transmission out of India;

(d)   in the case of a non-resident, being—
(1)   an individual who is not a citizen of India; or
(2)   a firm which does not have any partner who is a citizen of India or who is resident in India; or
(3)   a company which does not have any shareholder who is a citizen of India or who is resident in India,

no income shall be deemed to accrue or arise in India to such individual, firm or company through or from operations which are confined to the shooting of any cinematograph film in India;

Explanation 2 (as inserted by the Finance Act, 2003) provides that the expression "*business connection*" shall include a person acting on behalf of the non-resident, who, —

(a)   has and habitually exercises in India an authority to contract on behalf of the non-resident, unless his activities are limited to the purchase of goods or merchandise for the non-resident' or

(b) has no such authority, but habitually maintains in India a stock of goods or merchandise from which he regularly delivers goods or merchandise on behalf of the non-resident; or

(c) habitually secures orders in India, mainly or wholly for the non-resident or for that non-resident and other non-residents controlling, controlled by, or subject to the same common control, as that non-resident.

The "business connection", however, shall not be held to be established in cases where the non-resident carries on business through a broker, general commission agent or any other agent of an independent status, provided that such a person is acting in the ordinary course of his business.

It is further clarified that a broker, general commission agent or any other agent who does not work mainly or wholly on behalf of the non-resident or on behalf of that non-resident and other non-residents controlling, controlled by, or subject to the same common control, as that non-resident, shall be deemed to be a broker, general commission agent or an agent of an independent status.

(ii) income which falls under the head "Salaries", if it is earned in India.

Explanation—For the removal of doubts, it is hereby declared that the income of the nature referred to in this clause payable for—

    (a) service rendered in India; and

    (b) the rest period or leave period which is preceded and succeeded by services rendered in India and forms part of the service contract of employment,

    shall be regarded as income earned in India;

(iii) income chargeable under the head "Salaries" payable by the Government to a citizen of India for service outside India;

(iv) a dividend paid by an Indian company outside India;

(v) income by way of interest payable by—

    (a) the Government ; or

    (b) a person who is a resident, except where the interest is payable in respect of any debt incurred, or moneys borrowed and used, for the purposes of a business or profession carried on by such person outside India or for the purposes of making or earning any income from any source outside India; or

    (c) a person who is a non-resident, where the interest is payable in respect of any debt incurred, or moneys borrowed and used, for the purposes of a business or profession carried on by such person in India;

(vi) income by way of royalty payable by—

(a) the Government; or

(b) a person who is a resident, except where the royalty is payable in respect of any right, property or information used or services utilised for the purposes of a business or profession carried on by such person outside India or for the purposes of making or earning any income from any source outside India; or

(c) a person who is a non-resident, where the royalty is payable in respect of any right, property or information used or services utilised for the purposes of a business or profession carried on by such person in India or for the purposes of making or earning any income from any source in India:

Provided that nothing contained in this clause shall apply in relation to so much of the income by way of royalty as consists of lump sum consideration for the transfer outside India of, or the imparting of information outside India in respect of, any data, documentation, drawing or specification relating to any patent, invention, model, design, secret formula or process or trade mark or similar property, if such income is payable in pursuance of an agreement made before the 1st day of April, 1976, and the agreement is approved by the Central Government:

Provided further that nothing contained in this clause shall apply in relation to so much of the income by way of royalty as consists of lump sum payment made by a person, who is a resident, for the transfer of all or any rights (including the granting of a licence) in respect of computer software supplied by a non-resident manufacturer along with a computer or computer-based equipment under any scheme approved under the Policy on Computer Software Export, Software Development and Training, 1986 of the Government of India.

Explanation 1.—For the purposes of the first proviso, an agreement made on or after the 1st day of April, 1976, shall be deemed to have been made before that date if the agreement is made in accordance with proposals approved by the Central Government before that date; so, however, that, where the recipient of the income by way of royalty is a foreign company, the agreement shall not be deemed to have been made before that date unless, before the expiry of the time allowed under sub-section (1) or sub-section (2) of Section 139 (whether fixed originally or on extension) for furnishing the return of income for the assessment year commencing on the 1st day of April, 1977, or the assessment year in respect of which such income first becomes chargeable to tax under this Act, whichever assessment year is later, the company exercises an option by furnishing a declaration in writing to the Assessing Officer (such option being final for that assessment year and for every subsequent assessment year) that the agreement may be regarded as an agreement made before the 1st day of April, 1976.

Explanation 2.—For the purposes of this clause, "royalty" means consideration (including any lump sum consideration but excluding any consideration which would be the income of the recipient chargeable under the head "Capital gains") for—

(i)   the transfer of all or any rights (including the granting of a licence) in respect of a patent, invention, model, design, secret formula or process or trade mark or similar property;

(ii) the imparting of any information concerning the working of, or the use of, a patent, invention, model, design, secret formula or process or trade mark or similar property;

(iii) the use of any patent, invention, model, design, secret formula or process or trade mark or similar property;

(iv) the imparting of any information concerning technical, industrial, commercial or scientific knowledge, experience or skill;

(iva) the use or right to use, any industrial, commercial scientific equipment (inserted by the Finance Act, 2001).

(v)   the transfer of all or any rights (including the granting of a licence) in respect of any copyright, literary, artistic or scientific work including films or video tapes for use in connection with television or tapes for use in connection with radio broadcasting, but not including consideration for the sale, distribution or exhibition of cinematographic films; or

(vi) the rendering of any services in connection with the activities referred to in sub-clause (i) to (v).

Explanation 3.—For the purposes of this clause, "computer software" means any computer programme recorded on any disc, tape, perforated media or other information storage device and includes any such programme or any customized electronic data;

(vii) income by way of fees for technical service payable by—

(a)   the Government ; or

(b)   a person who is a resident, except where the fees are payable in respect of services utilised in a business or profession carried on by such person outside India or for the purposes of making or earning any income from any source outside India; or

(c)   a person who is a non-resident, where the fees are payable in respect of services utilised in a business or profession carried on by such person in India or for the purposes of making or earning any income from any source in India:

Provided that nothing contained in this clause shall apply in relation to any income by way of fees for technical services payable in pursuance of an agreement made before the 1st day of April 1976, and approved by the Central Government.

Explanation 1.—For the purposes of the foregoing proviso, an agreement made on or after the 1st day of April, 1976, shall be deemed to have been made before that date if the agreement is made in accordance with proposals approved by the Central Government before that date.

Explanation 2.—For the purposes of this clause, "fees for technical services" means any consideration (including any lump sum consideration) for the rendering of any managerial, technical or consultancy services (including the provision of services of technical or other personnel) but does not include consideration for any construction, assembly, mining or like project undertaken by the recipient or consideration which would be income of the recipient chargeable under the head "Salaries".

(2) Notwithstanding anything contained in sub-section (1), any pension payable outside India to a person residing permanently outside India shall not be deemed to accrue or arise in India, if the pension is payable to a person referred to in article 314 of the Constitution or to a person who, having been appointed before the 15th day of August, 1947, to be a Judge of the Federal Court or of a High Court within the meaning of the Government of India Act, 1935, continues to serve on or after the commencement of the Constitution as a Judge in India.

Explanation — For the removal of doubts, it is hereby declared that for the purposes of this section, where income is deemed to accrue or arise in India under clauses (v), (vi) and (vii) of sub-section (1), such income shall be included in the total income of the non-resident, whether or not the non-resident has a residence or place or business or business connection in India.

(This Explanation has been inserted by the Finance Act, 2007, retrospectively from 1.6.1976)

Similarly, there is no income tax in India on a foreign income merely because it is remitted to India during that year. In the case of a person who is resident but not ordinarily resident in India within the meaning of Section 6(6) of the Income Tax Act as explained in Chapter 1, topic 5, no income tax is payable by him on the income which accrues or arises to him outside India unless it is derived from a business controlled, or any profession set up, in India. It is only a resident and ordinarily resident person who is liable to pay income tax in India on Indian income as well as foreign income. Hence for the purpose of adoption of proper tax planning by a non-resident person in general and a non-resident Indian in particular, it would be advisable

---

Illustration No. 18

R is a non-resident in India for the financial year 2007-2008 relevant to the assessment year 2008-2009. His Indian income is Rs. 1,60,000 only. Besides, he has earned a sum of Rs. 12,00,000 in Hong Kong. R is liable to income tax in India only on the Indian income of Rs. 1,60,000. The foreign income of Rs. 12,00,000 is not liable to tax in India.

Illustration No. 19

S has received a sum of Rs. 29,50,000 as salary in New York. He remits Rs. 14,60,000 out of this salary to India. He has no other income in India. He is non-resident in India for the financial year 2006-2007. On these facts he will not be liable to any tax in India because there is no income tax on remittances of foreign income.

Illustration No. 20

T is resident but not ordinarily resident in India for the financial year 2007-2008 relevant for the Assessment Year 2008-2009. He controls a business set up in New York from his Head Office in New Delhi. The income from this business is Rs. 1,60,000. Besides, the interest on income received or accruing to T in a foreign country is Rs. 2,40,000. On these facts, no income tax is payable on the sum of Rs. 2,40,000 received or accruing to T outside India. However, he would be liable to pay income tax on Rs. 1,60,000 from a foreign business controlled from India.

for him to see that he remains a non-resident for at least nine years consecutively so that for the coming year even if he becomes a resident person in India, he is treated as a resident but not ordinarily resident person, thereby enabling him to claim full exemption on the foreign income earned by him or accruing to him or received by him outside India, as has been explained in Chapter 1, topic 9. These provisions of law governing the scope of total income of a non-resident Indian are explained below by means of a few examples.

4. Income tax liability of an NRI

The income tax liability of a non-resident Indian is not dependent upon his citizenship in India or any other country. Thus a citizen as well as a non-citizen will be taxed alike in respect of their income in India. The income tax liability, however, varies great deal on the difference in the residential status of different individuals. As stated in the preceding para, a non-resident or a non-resident Indian is liable to income tax in India only on the Indian income. No income tax is payable in India on a total income up to Rs. 1,00,000 during the financial year relevant to the assessment year A.Y. 2006-2007 and A.Y. 2007-2008. From the A.Y. 2008-2009, this exemption limit is increased to 1,10,000. Total income is computed after adding income from different sources in India and subtracting the various deductions admissible under the different provisions of the Income Tax Act. It is the resultant income which is treated as total income or taxable income for the purpose of computation of income tax liability in the case of a non-resident Indian, in the same manner as in regard to a resident individual. The Finance Act, 2007 among other things lays down the rates of income tax on individuals. These rates are different for different slabs of income.

The following rates of income-tax would be applicable on the total income of a non-resident Indian for the financial year 2005-2006 relevant to A.Y. 2006-2007 as well as for the financial year 2006-2007 relevant to the Assessment Year 2007-2008:

(1)	On total income upto Rs. 1,00,000	Nil
(2)	On total income between Rs. 1,00,000 and Rs. 1,50,000	10%
(3)	On total income between Rs. 1,50,000 and Rs. 2,50,000	20%
(4)	On total income in excess Rs. 2,50,000	30%

The income-tax is to be increased by an educational cess of 2% on the tax payable, plus a surcharge @10% for individuals and HUFs having more than Rs. 10 lakh total income. The exemption limit for *resident* women tax payers, however, is Rs. 1,35,000; while for *resident* senior citizens it is Rs. 1,85,000. Higher exemption limit for non-resident women tax payers as well as for non-resident senior citizens is not available.

As per the Finance Act, 2007 the following rates of income tax would be applicable on the total income of a non-resident Indian for the financial year 2007-2008 relevant to the Assessment Year 2008-2009:

(1) On total income up to Rs. 1,10,000   Nil
(2) On total income between Rs. 1,10,000 & Rs. 1,50,000   10%
(3) On total income between Rs. 1,50,000 & Rs. 2,50,000   20%
(4) On total income in excess of Rs. 2,50,000   30%

The income-tax is to be increased by two cases:

(a) 2% of the income tax as Educational Cess
(b) 1% of the income tax as Secondary & Higher Education Cess.

There is a surcharge of 10% on income tax on total income in excess of Rs. 10 lakh.

The exemption limit for *resident* women taxpayers is Rs. 1,45,000 while for *resident* senior citizens it is Rs. 1,95,000.

Where a particular income is totally exempt from income tax, it does not form part of the total income and is not even included for any purpose whatsoever. A list of such exemptions are given in Section 10 of the Income Tax Act. A detailed list of such income, is given in Chapter 4. Besides, there are certain expenses or other deductions which are allowed from the gross income to arrive at the net taxable income. See Chapter 8.

The above slab rates of income tax are applicable to the non-resident Indians in general as well as residents. A special procedure in the matter of computation of income tax in respect of certain incomes of non-resident Indians has also been laid down in the Income Tax Act. A non-resident Indian can opt to have the special procedure of calculation of income tax in respect of some special sources of income. This is described in detail in Chapter 7. The computation of income tax liability in the case of a non-resident Indian is explained by means of a few examples given below.

Illustration No. 21

The following are the sources of income of U, a non-resident Indian in India for the Assessment Year 2008-2009:

1. Net income from house property	Rs. 67,000
2. Bank interest & Interest on Govt. Securities	Rs. 50,000
3. Interest on deposit in non-resident (External) account in a bank in India	Rs. 10,000

For calculating U's total income tax liability, we first need to calculate his total taxable income.

1. Income from house property (net)	Rs. 67,000
2. Bank interest & interest on government securities [No deduction now]	Rs. 50,000
3. Interest on Deposit in a Non resident (External) account in a bank, completely exempt from income tax under Section 10(4A) of the I. T. Act	Nil
4. Total income	Rs. 1,17,000

The income tax payable by U on his total (taxable) income in India of Rs. 1,17,000 will be computed as follows:

1. Income tax on the first Rs. 1,10,000	Nil
2. Income tax on the next Rs. 7,000 @ 10 %	Rs. 700
3. Education cess @ 2% of tax payable	Rs. 14
4. Secondary & Higher Education Cess @1%	Rs. 7
5. Total income tax payable by U	Rs. 721

Illustration No. 22

The only source of income of V, a non-resident Indian, is interest on bank fixed deposits held by him in India and is Rs. 1,64,000. For the financial year 2007-2008 relevant to the Assessment Year 2008-2009. The same will be taxable.

Illustration No. 23

X, a non-resident Indian, has the following sources of income in India in respect of different periods as given below :

(a) Rs. 90,000 income from house property (net) for the financial year 2007-2008;

(b) Rs. 30,000 profit and gains of a cloth business set up in August 2007 for the previous year ending on 31 March 2008.

The total income of X for the previous year 2007-2008 relevant to the assessment year 2008-2009 will be only Rs. 1,20,000.

5. Significance of the Assessment Year and Previous Year

The assessment of a non-resident Indian (like a resident person) is made in terms of a particular period which is known as assessment year. Under Section 2(9) of the Income Tax Act 1961 the expression "assessment year" means the period of twelve months commencing on the first day of April every year. The present assessment year is 2007-2008. Thus, the next assessment year is 2008-2009. It means the period of 12 months commencing on 1 April 2007 and ending on 31 March 2008. Whenever any return of income is to be filed by a non-resident Indian in relation to the assessment year 2007-2008, it would have to be filed in relation to and generally within the period 1 April 2007 to 31 March 2008. It is not the income earned during this period which is subject to assessment. It is only the basis of assessment in relation to a particular year which gives special significance to the expression "assessment year". It is the income of a non-resident Indian of a particular previous year which is liable to income tax in India. The term "previous year" is spoken of in relation to the term "assessment year". Income tax is leviable annually for each financial year whereas income tax is to be paid on the income of the previous financial year which is technically known as previous year. Thus, income is made in one financial year and income tax thereon is levied in the following financial year. The previous year is also known as the accounting year or income year of a taxpayer including a non-resident Indian and means the 12 months ending on the 31st March immediately preceding the assessment year. Thus, for the assessment year 2007-2008 the previous year would be the financial year 2006-2007 and for the A.Y. 2008-2009, the previous year would be the financial year 2007-2008.

6. Income tax incidence on a non-resident partnership firm, a non-resident HUF or a non-resident company

We have seen in Chapter 1, para 10, the various provisions of the Income Tax Act in the matter of determination of residential status of a partnership firm or a Hindu undivided family or a company. The exemption limit in the case of a Hindu undivided families is also Rs. 1,10,000 like in the case of an individual for the assessment year 2008-2009.

A partnership firm is liable to tax at the rate of 30%. These provisions not being of general use for non-resident Indians are not discussed here in this book.

A non-resident company is liable to pay income tax on its total income @ 40%. Certain special incomes of a non-resident company from royalty and technical service fees are, however, liable to tax at certain concessional rates of income tax @ 20% in most cases.

7. The heads of income liable to tax in India

The various heads of income chargeable to income tax in India in the case of a non-resident Indian (as well as resident taxpayers) are as follows:

(1)	Salaries	Sections 15 to 17
(2)	Income from house property	Sections 22 to 27
(3)	Profits and gains of business or profession	Sections 28 to 44D
(4)	Capital gains	Sections 45 to 55
(5)	Income from other sources	Sections 56 to 59

30% of the annual value of house property is allowed as a deductible expense in computing taxable income from house property. Besides, interest on borrowings for investment in rental housing is deductible. However, such interest should not exceed Rs. 1,50,000 p.a. in the case of a self-occupied house.

8. How to compute the taxable income of a non-resident Indian

In the preceding para 4 we have discussed the provisions of the Income Tax Act in the matter of computation of income tax liability of a non-resident Indian. Here, we shall specifically deal with the steps which are necessary for the computation of the total income or taxable income of a non-resident Indian in relation to a particular assessment year. The first step in computation of the total income is under each head of income separately after making the specified deductions and taking into account allowances allowed in computing income under such head of income. The total of the income under different heads of income is known as the gross total income. Any income which is completely exempt from tax (see Chapter 4) is not to form part of the gross total income. Certain deductions in the matter of investment in Bank deposits, etc., (see Chapter 7) are allowed from the gross total income. The balance is the taxable income of the non-resident Indian and is technically known as the "total income" of the non-resident Indian for a previous year in relation to a particular assessment year. A deduction of income tax is allowed on the investment in the form of NSCs (VIII Issue), P.P.F., special units, bonds, etc., under Section 80C of the Income Tax Act. This is explained by means of an example given below.

Illustration No. 24

Y, a non-resident Indian, has income under the following heads during the previous year 2007-2008 relevant to the assessment year 2008-2009:

		Rs.
(a)	Gross salary from an Indian concern for two months	1,60,000
(b)	Net rent (less municipal tax on house property)	30,000
(c)	Interest on RBI Relief Bonds	25,000
(d)	Interest on bank fixed deposit and government securities	38,000

The total income of Y for the assessment year 2008-2009 would be computed as follows:

(a)	Gross Salary	1,60,000	
	(No Standard deduction)		
	[Nil from the A.Y. 2006-07]	———	60,000

Contd...

		Rs.	Rs.
(b)	Income from house property rent	30,000	
	Less: 30% for repairs, etc. under Section 24 (1) (i)	9,000	21,000
(c)	Interest on Relief Bonds (fully exempt)	25,000	—
(d)	Gross interest on bank fixed deposit, etc.	38,000	
	(Deduction under Section 80L is not available from the A.Y. 2006-07)		38,000
	Total income of Y for the assessment year 2008-2009		2,19,000

The following are some of the most important points which should be remembered by an NRI in computing the (taxable) total income:

(a) If there is loss from one source of income, it can be set off against income from another source under the same head of income as per Section 70 of the I.T. Act. If there is a short-term capital loss, it can be set off against short-term capital gain or long-term capital gain regarding any capital asset in the same assessment year. But the long-term capital loss can be set off only against taxable long-term capital gain and not against short-term capital gain.

(b) Normally, the loss under one head of income can be set off against income under another head of income except (i) business loss which cannot be set off against income under the head "Salaries", and (ii) loss under the head "Capital gains", as per Section 71 of the I.T. Act, 1961.

(c) Loss under the head "Income from house property" which can not be set off as described in (b) above shall be allowed to be carried forward for the next 8 assessment years for set off against income from house property as per Section 71B of the I.T. Act, 1961.

(d) Unabsorbed business loss can be carried forward for set off against income under the head "Profits and gains of business or profession" for the next 8 assessment years as per Section 72 of the I.T. Act. However, speculation losses can be set off or carried forward and set off for the next 8 years only against speculation profits, as per Section 73 of the I.T. Act.

(e) The unabsorbed short-term capital loss can be carried forward for set off against any capital gain — both long-term and short-term for the next 8 assessment years. However, long–term capital loss can be carried forward and set off for the next 8 assessment years only against long-term capital gain, as per Section 74 of the I.T. Act.

(f) The above rules are relevant for the computation of Indian taxable income and are not to be affected by the gain or loss made by the NRI in the foreign country.

9. Income tax planning by an NRI returning to India permanently

As discussed earlier and also in Chapter 4 of this book, an NRI can enjoy complete exemption from income-tax while remaining an NRI and thus, he need not pay any income-tax under the Income Tax Act in India. However, NRIs deciding to return to India on a permanent basis are often perplexed as to the tax planning to be adopted by them to be able to have zero income tax level for their earnings in India. One important point that should be remembered by an NRI returning to India on a permanent basis is that his income, like interest on non-resident (external) account which was completely exempt when he was an NRI would no longer be so exempt when he returns to India. However, in respect of his foreign income on the investment allowed by the RBI to be kept abroad, he would not be liable to tax in India so long as he remains a resident but not ordinarily resident in India. The precautions to be taken in this regard have been explained in detail in Chapter 1, Topic 9. But if an NRI carries on any business abroad while remaining a resident in India, he would not be liable to tax thereon in India. However, a zero tax liability can be obtained by an NRI returning to India on Indian income by adopting proper tax planning in respect of his investment in his name as well as in the names of his family members.

One important aspect that should be taken care of by a returning NRI is that there should be sufficient investment in the names of the spouse and major children. Besides, a new file in the name of Hindu undivided family can also be started by the returning NRI. The investment should be made in each of the files in such a manner that the amount of taxable income is kept below exemption limit, which at present is Rs. 1,00,000 and Rs. 1,10,000 from the Assessment Year 2008-2009. Every returning NRI must adopt tax planning carefully so as to avoid clubbing of the income of his spouse or daughter-in-law or minor children with his income. For this purpose, he should go through the detailed hints given in Chapter 3 of this book. Likewise, an NRI can make investments through the help of well-known brokers in shares of reputed companies so that there is security along with liquidity of investment and the dividend income is eligible to exemption under Section 10(34) from income tax, as is explained in Chapter 4 of the book. The investment may also be made in mutual funds as the income from mutual funds is exempt from tax.

If there is any taxable income, say on account of rental income or investment in non-banking deposits, etc., then the tax incidence can be reduced through investments in PPF, NSCs, Life Insurance premiums, specified and notified infrastructure bonds, units, etc. under Section 80C where from the A.Y. 2006-07 deduction from income is allowed upto a maximum investment of Rs. 1,00,000 per tax-payer, as is explained in detail in Chapter 8.

Where an NRI is interested in having a house, he can invest his funds in the purchase or construction of a self-occupied residential house, the income of which will be nil for income tax purposes. Further, he can even borrow moneys from his relative and get a deduction on interest upto Rs. 1,50,000 every year from any other taxable income. The above account of tax planning to be adopted by an NRI gives the most important aspects of tax planning to achieve a zero income tax level. For greater exemption on higher income a returning NRI would do well to refer to the various topics in Chapters 4, 5 and 8 of this book.

10. Wealth tax liability of an NRI?

Wealth tax is payable in India under the Wealth Tax Act 1957 on net wealth as on a particular date, which is known as the valuation date. Generally speaking, valuation date is the last day of the previous year i.e., 31 March. The expression "previous year" has been explained in para 5 earlier. Wealth tax is payable by individuals and Hindu undivided families and certain companies. A non-resident individual in India, like any other resident individual is liable to wealth tax only when the net wealth on taxable "assets" on a valuation date exceeds Rs. 15 lakh. The amount of Rs. 15 lakh excludes certain exemptions from wealth tax, the details of which have been described in Chapter 6. From the total value of taxable wealth, deduction is allowed in respect of debts and liabilities. The items of wealth which are either totally exempt from wealth tax and or which are so exempt from wealth tax up to a particular limit are deducted from the gross wealth to arrive at the taxable wealth on the valuation date. Generally speaking, the value of assets on the valuation date as per III Schedule to the Wealth Tax Act is taken for the purpose of computation of wealth tax payable by a non-resident individual. Hence, a non-resident should so plan his investments in India that he secures the maximum deductions and exemptions in a manner that he is liable to least possible wealth tax. The rate of wealth tax for the assessment years 1993-94 to 2008-2009 in the case of a non-resident individual(as also in the case of a resident individual) is 1% of the taxable net wealth.

A non-resident Indian is liable to wealth tax in India on his Indian wealth and not on his foreign wealth (see Chapter 6 for details). The liability of a non-resident Indian to wealth tax in India is explained by means of certain examples given below.

Illustration No. 25

Z, a non-resident Indian, has bought urban land and jewellery worth Rs. 20 lakh. He has Rs. 40 lakh in bank deposit and other bank accounts, as on 31 March 2007. The wealth tax payable by Z on the net wealth as on the valuation date of 31 March 2007 relevant to the assessment year 2007-2008 will be computed only on Rs. 20 lakh – Rs. 15 lakh (exempted), i.e. on Rs. 5 lakh as the amount of Rs. 40 lakh, being deposits in bank is exempt. The wealth tax computed @ 1% on Rs. 5 lakh = Rs. 5,000.

Illustration No. 26

Y, a non-resident Indian and a citizen of India has the following investments in India as on 31 March 2007:

	Rs.
(a) House property on rent for 250 days	4,00,000
(b) Shares in Indian companies	7,00,00C
(c) 6.5% Savings Bonds	8,00,000
(d) Jewellery and cash in hand	9,00,000

Contd...

The net wealth liable to wealth tax in India of
Y, a non-resident Indian will first be computed as :
Jewellery and cash in hand
    & rented house property   Rs. 13,00,000
(The other items of wealth are completely exempt from wealth tax.)

As the net wealth does not exceed Rs. 15 lakh, no wealth tax is payable by Y on his wealth in India.

---

11. Conclusion

The foregoing discussions on the preliminary aspects of taxation particularly in relation to tax liability in the previous year of a non-resident Indian, are of a special significance for determining the true income tax incidence in India by adoption of proper tax planning, both in the matter of complete exemption from income tax in India by becoming a non-resident or by investing the funds in a manner that the maximum exemption from income tax and wealth tax is available to him.

CHAPTER 3

How an NRI can avoid clubbing of his income and wealth with that of his spouse and children

1. Introduction

A non-resident Indian has to plan gifts in such a manner that there is no clubbing of income and/wealth of wife and children with the income of the husband or father. Normally, a person who is the owner of a particular asset is liable to income tax on its income. Similarly, the owner of wealth is alone liable to wealth tax in India. But there are certain clubbing provisions both under the Income Tax Act and the Wealth Tax Act which aim at preventing transfer of funds or gifts of moneys to very close relations like wife, and children. For example, if proper tax planning is not adopted, the income of wife out of gifts made by the husband would be liable to be clubbed together with the income of the husband, frustrating the purpose of gift from the point of view of tax planning. Likewise, such a gift would also be clubbed with the wealth of the husband under the provisions of Section 4 of the Wealth Tax Act. Similarly, there are other clubbing provisions in relation to certain other close relatives. It is, therefore, very important to adopt proper tax planning so that a non-resident Indian makes gifts or adopts such tax planning in the matter of gift and settlement, etc. that the income of one member of the family is not added to the income of another member of the family. In this chapter we have discussed all the provisions the knowledge of which would enable the non-resident Indian to avoid clubbing of income and wealth of husband, wife and children in one hand.

2. Income from joint accounts or joint investments: Is it liable to be clubbed for tax purposes?

Very often it is found that a non-resident maintains a bank account jointly with his wife and/or children. Similarly, it is seen that a non-resident Indian buying shares or debentures or house property or other movable or immovable property, keeps them in his own name jointly with his wife or any other member of the family. In this connection, a non-resident should remember that the maintenance of joint bank accounts or holding of joint investments alone would not make the income liable to assessment separately in the hands of the persons in whose name the joint accounts are kept or who hold the joint investments. Thus, the mere fact that an account is held jointly or that an investment is held by two or more persons together would not affect the liability to income tax or wealth tax. The main criterion of deciding as to the correct persons who are to be responsible for paying income tax in respect of the income of joint accounts or joint investments is the true ownership of such accounts or investments. For example, if a non-resident Indian, out of money belonging to him, is operating a bank account or a bank fixed deposit account jointly with his wife, he alone would be liable to income tax, if any, in respect of the income from such an account. Likewise, if a non-resident Indian out of funds belonging to him makes a joint investment in shares of Indian companies, he alone, would he liable to income tax, if any, in respect of the dividend income from shares so held. If, however, a joint bank account or joint investment is out of money belonging to the persons actually owning the funds, then the extent of their individual ownership in the joint account would be considered for income tax and wealth tax for individual tax purposes separately.

For example, if a non-resident Indian invests Rs. 4,00,000 in the HUDCO Bonds, and his wife invests Rs. 2,00,000 out of funds belonging to her in buying HUDCO Bonds and these Bonds worth Rs. 6,00,000 are held in joint names of the husband and the wife, the income on such Bonds would be liable to be treated separately in the individual assessment of the husband and the wife in the ratio of 2:1.

3. When is the income of wife liable to be clubbed with the income of her husband, and *vice versa*?

Under the provisions of Section 64(1) of the Income Tax Act there are various situations under which the income of a wife is not considered for tax purposes in her own hand but is liable to be clubbed or added with the income of her husband. In certain situations the income of the husband could be clubbed with the income of the wife under the provisions of Section 64(1). Hence, a non-resident should adopt proper tax planning with a view to avoiding such clubbing of income. For doing so, it is necessary to understand the relevant provisions of Section 64(1) as given below so that such clubbing can be avoided altogether by non-resident Indians.

(a) Under the provision of Section 64(1)(iii) the salary, commission, fees or other forms of remuneration, whether in cash or in kind, received by the wife of a non-resident Indian from a concern in which the non-resident Indian has a substantial interest would be liable to be added to the income of the non-resident Indian. However, this provision would not apply if the wife possesses technical or professional qualifications and the income is solely attributable to the application of her technical or professional knowledge and experience. In the case of a company, if equity share carrying 20% or more of voting power at any time during the previous year are owned beneficially by the non-resident Indian or by him along with one or more of his relatives, the non-resident Indian would be deemed to have a substantial interest in the company. In any other case, like an association of persons or a partnership firm, non-resident Indian would be considered to have a substantial interest in the concern if he, along with one or more of his relatives, is entitled in the aggregate at any time during the previous year to 20% or more of the profits of such a concern. Hence, whenever a non-resident and his relatives are substantially interested in a concern, he should avoid paying any remuneration to his wife, unless the wife is technically or professionally qualified. If this precaution is not taken, then the remuneration so paid to the wife would be added to the income of the non-resident. This is equally applicable in the case of the wife where she is substantially interested in the concern and pays some remuneration to her husband who is not technically or professionally qualified.

(b) Under the provisions of Section 64(1)(iv) if a husband makes any gift to his wife, the income from such gift would be liable to be added his income. Similarly, in the case of wife. Where, however, a transfer of money or funds or assets takes place from the husband to the wife or vice versa for an adequate consideration, this provision would not apply. Another situation in which this provision is not applicable is where the transfer of assets or gifts is made in connection with an agreement to live apart. Hence, a non-resident should never make any gift to his wife so that he can avoid the clubbing of income from gifted assets in his own hands. If, however, the gift is made by a husband to his wife before marriage, then this provision would not apply.

(c) Another provision in the matter of clubbing of income of the husband and wife is Section 64(1)(vii) under which a gift made to any other person or to the trustees of a trust for the benefit of the spouse of a non-resident Indian would be liable to be clubbed in the hands of the donor spouse. Hence, a non-resident Indian should not only refrain from making a gift directly to his wife but should also not make any gift indirectly in favour of the trustees of a trust for the benefit of his wife, so that the clubbing of income arising to the wife out of assets so gifted by the husband to the wife is avoided. This provision is equally applicable in the case of a gift by the wife to a trust for the benefit of the husband.

4. When is the income of a minor child liable to be clubbed with that of a parent?

The provisions relating to the clubbing of income of a minor child with the income of the parent or the grand-parent, as the case may be, have undergone a great deal of change due after the amendments made to Section 64, by the Finance Act, 1992, with effect from the Assessment Year 1993-94. Under the provisions of Section 64 (1A) as inserted by the Finance Act, 1992, with effect from the Assessment Year 1993-94 in computing the total income of any individual, whether a resident or a non-resident, the entire income accruing to his minor child would be clubbed i.e., included in that income. Thus the income of the minor child from gifts made by any one and not necessarily the parents or grand-parents only, by way of interest income or rental income, etc., on investments made out of the funds of the minor child would be clubbed with the income of the parent.

However, the clubbing provision would not apply if the income of the minor child accrues or arises on account of any

a) manual work done by him; or

b) activity involving application of his skill, talent, or specialised knowledge and experience.

Thus if a grown up child aged, say 14 or 15, earns some income out of the exercise of his special talent in computer science, games, sports, shorthand, etc., the income so derived by the minor would not be clubbed with the income of his or her parent.

The Finance Act, 1994 had, with effect from the Assessment Year 1995-96, provided that the clubbing provisions of Section 64(1A) would not apply in the case of a disabled child suffering from any disability of the nature mentioned in Section 80-U.

The question may be asked to the particular parent with whose income the income of the minor has to be included. For this purpose, it is provided that where the marriage of the parents of a minor child subsists, then the clubbing has to be done with the income of that parent whose total income, excluding the income under Section 64(1A), is greater. Where, however, the marriage of the parents does not subsist, then the clubbing has to be done with the income of that parent who maintains the minor child in that previous year. Further, while any such income is once included in the total income of her one parent, any such income arising in any succeeding year would not be included in the total income of the other parent, unless the Assessing Officer is satisfied, after giving that parent an opportunity of being heard, that it is necessary to do so.

Under the provisions of Section 10(32) of the Income Tax Act complete exemption is enjoyed by the parent in respect of the income of the minor child so included to the extent of Rs. 1,500 for each minor child.

A minor can, however, now be admitted to the benefits of partnership in a partnership firm even where his father or mother is a partner, without invoking the clubbing provisions of Section 64. Thus, with effect from the Assessment Year 1993-94 the share income of a minor child on his being admitted to the benefits of the partnership will not be clubbed with the income of the father or the mother but would be completely exempt from income tax under provisions of Section 10(2A). Hence proper tax planning can be adopted in respect of the funds of the minor child so as to prevent the clubbing of the income of the minor child with that of his parent by admitting the minor child, wherever it is possible, in a partnership firm. In such a case the entire share income received by the minor would be completely exempt from income tax and there would not be any scope of clubbing such share income with that of the parent. Likewise, if the minor has any income which is completely exempt from income tax under the provisions of Section 10, like interest on deposits in PPF account, etc., the clubbing provisions of Section 64(1A) are not applicable simply because such income is fully exempt from income tax.

5. When is the income of daughter-in-law liable to be clubbed with that of her father-in-law or mother-in-law?

Normally, every major person in India is entitled to have income in his own hands in such a manner that he is liable to pay income tax thereon in his own individual assessment. There is a provision of clubbing of income arising to the daughter-in-law which can sometimes be clubbed with the income of the father-in-law or the mother-in-law. Thus, it is provided in Section 64(1)(vi) that if the daughter-in-law receives any gift from the father-in-law or mother-in-law, the income arising out of or in relation to such gifts is considered as the income not of the daughter-in-law, but of the father-in-law or the mother-in-law making the gift. Thus, the father-in-law or the mother-in-law should never make any gift to his or her daughter-in-law. Likewise, no gift should be made in favour of any trust for the benefit of the daughter-in-law by the father-in-law or the mother-in-law. Otherwise, under the provisions of Section 64(1)(viii) such income, which is for the immediate or deferred benefit of the son's wife, would be liable to be clubbed with the income of the father-in-law or the mother-in-law so making the gift. Hence, whenever the father-in-law or the mother-in-law of a non-resident Indian, like any other Indian, wishes to make a gift out of love and affection to their daughter-in-law they should refrain from exercising such love through the medium of gift. The gift may be made by any other relative, like her maternal uncle, paternal uncle, her father, her mother, her brother, or the uncle-in-law or aunt-in-law, grand-father-in-law or grand mother-in-law. In topic 3 above, we have seen that income out of gift made by the husband to the wife and vice versa is liable to be clubbed together. Hence a married woman should not receive any gift from three persons, namely, her husband, her father-in-law, and her mother-in-law, so as to avoid the risk of clubbing of income under the provisions of Section 64(1). It should be carefully noted by a non-resident Indian that he should not make any such gifts to his daughter-in-law even when he is outside India because when such money is brought into India by the daughter-in-law, it is liable to be clubbed with the income of the non-resident Indian when he returns to India. Thus, for the purposes of tax planning by a non-resident Indian, this aspect should be kept in mind so that the non-resident Indian after his return to India is not saddled with the additional burden of paying income tax on the income earned by the daughter-in-law out of gifts made by him in the past.

6. Income of a major child cannot be clubbed with that of his parent

A person becomes a major on the completion of 18 years. Thus at any time during any previous year if a person becomes a major, he is considered to be a major for the entire period of the previous year and not necessarily in respect of the income earned after the date of attainment of majority. This is an important aspect which should be kept in view by a taxpayer for the adoption of tax planning in the case of those minor children who are likely to attain majority in a particular year. However, if there is any income of a major child, whether son or daughter, even out of gifts made by NRI or anyone else, the clubbing provision of Section 64 would not apply. The entire income of the major child would be assessed separately and independently in the hands of the major child only.

7. When is the income of an HUF from self-converted assets liable to be clubbed in the members' hands?

An individual governed by the Mitakshara school of Hindu law is entitled to convert his self-acquired property through his unilateral action of impressing such self-acquired property or separate property with the character of property belonging to an HUF or throw it to the common pot of the HUF. But such an action is not viewed favourably by the Income Tax Law. It is provided in Section 64(2) that when any individual, who is a member of a Hindu undivided family convert his self-acquired property at any time after 31.12.1969 into HUF property, for the proposes of computation of the total income of such individual the income from the converted property is to be deemed to arise to the individual and not to the family. Because of the clubbing provision it is generally not advantageous for a Hindu to convert his self-acquired property into HUF property. Rather, the HUF may receive gifts from non-members of the HUF. In the latter case, the clubbing provision would not apply. However, where a full partition is desired and several Hindu undivided families are to be formed by the full partition, it may be effected amongst the members of the family. Then each unit, headed by the major eldest male member with his own wife, and children, will be deemed to constitute a separate HUF. The individual who converts his self-acquired property into HUF property is deemed to have transferred indirectly his property to his spouse or minor child. The property allotted on partition to the major members of the family is not considered to be indirectly transferred by him to them and hence, the clubbing provision after partition does not apply in respect of such partition of the converted assets. A non-resident Indian, can take advantage of this aspect of tax planning in those cases where he has grown up children who are in turn married and have their separate branches of HUF and where there is no separate HUF file for them.

8. When is income from assets received on partial partition of an HUF liable to be clubbed with the income of the HUF?

One of the important methods of tax planning in India has been to make a partial partition of the assets of an HUF so that the income of the family is divided amongst various hands in such a manner that the least income tax is paid by the HUF and the members of the HUF taken together. Hence, partial partition of an HUF after 31.12.1978 has been de-recognised. It is provided in Section 171 (9) of the Income Tax Act that where a partial partition takes place amongst the members of a Hindu undivided family after 31.12.1978, such a family shall continue to be liable to be assessed under the Income Tax Act as if no such partial partition had taken place. Further, each member or group of members of such a family immediately before such partial partition and the HUF shall be jointly and severally liable for any tax, penalty, interest, fine or any other sum payable under the Income Tax Act by the family in respect of any period, whether before or after such partial partition. Hence, tax planning requires that there should not be any partial partition of a Hindu undivided family. If at all partition becomes necessary, then full partition under the provisions of Section 171 may be made amongst the different members of the family. Thus, from the point of view of proper tax planning a non-resident Indian like any other resident person should never make a partial partition of the assets of his undivided family of which he may be the Karta or Manager. Rather, if he has major sons in the family he may make full partition of the family so that his major sons in turn may have their independent and separate HUFs.

9. Joint ownership of house property: Does it make the income of a husband, wife, and children liable to be clubbed together?

A non-resident Indian is not liable to pay income tax on the full income from any property jointly owned by him with his wife. The only precaution that he should take is that there is no gift made by him to his wife. If this precaution is taken, the joint ownership of movable as well as immovable assets will entitle each of the owner to claim separate income tax assessment in his or her hands independently. Thus, a non-Indian resident could own shares of a limited company out of money belonging to him as well as out of separate funds belonging to his wife as also the funds of a major child. Thus, if the shares in a limited company are owned in three names with the funds contributed by the three persons as mentioned earlier, each of the persons would be liable to be taxed separately and not be clubbed together. In particular, this provision is recognised for the purpose of joint ownership of house property. Thus, it is provided in Section 26 that where property consisting of building or buildings and lands appertaining thereto is owned by two or more than two persons and their respective shares are definite and ascertainable, such persons in respect of such property are not to be assessed as an association of persons, but the share of each person in the income from the property would be included in his total income separately. In the case of other investment, like shares, debentures, etc., there is sometimes a risk of joint investment being considered as the investment of an association of persons. In the interest of avoiding confusion and clubbing of income, a non-resident Indian should not make joint investments for movable assets. But as regards immovable house property, because of the clear cut provision contained in Section 26 there is no risk if it is purchased out of separate and independent funds belonging to the husband, wife and the major children, namely, all of them together, and it would not be liable to be clubbed. Rather, the income of each co-owner would be liable to separate assessment independently. This aspect of tax planning can be taken care of while purchasing house property, particularly where the house property is big and saving of income tax and wealth tax becomes important.

10. How to avoid clubbing of the wife's wealth with that of the husband's

The provisions of clubbing of income of certain close relatives for the purpose of income tax, as discussed are equally relevant for the purposes of wealth tax. Hence, a non-resident Indian, like any other resident person, should so adopt proper tax planning that there is no clubbing of wealth of his wife with his own wealth. Thus, he should refrain from making any gift whether out of assets outside India or assets in India to his wife. That is why the wife of the non-resident Indian should also not make any gift of any assets, whether out of funds in India or funds outside India to her husband. Likewise, the non-resident Indian should not make any gift of any property in favour of the daughter-in-law or to any trust in favour of or for the benefit of the daughter-in-law. If these precautions are taken, the gifted assets are not to be clubbed with the assets of the person making the gift under the provisions of Section 4(1) of the Wealth Tax Act. This aspect of tax planning is very relevant for saving wealth tax and particularly for saving oneself from the clubbing provisions of wealth tax. Of course, the taxable wealth of a minor child would be clubbed with the wealth of the NRI under Section 4(1) of the Wealth Tax Act from the Assessment Year 1993-94. Usually, it is seen that a non-resident transfers certain amount of money out of his own funds in favour of his wife and minor children, under the impression that each one of them would be liable to wealth tax independently. In particular he is under the impression that for seven years there is complete exemption of the assets from the payment of wealth tax if he returns to India permanently. Though this is true, after the end of the seven-year period the transferred assets in favour of wife and minor children would be liable to be clubbed for the purposes of wealth tax in his hands.

11. Gift from non-relatives now taxed as income

If you receive a gift then please be a little careful specially in view of the new amendment introduced by the Finance (No. 2) Act, 2004 whereby a gift received on and after 1-9-2004 from a non-relative would be treated as income and taxed accordingly. However, these provisions would not apply in respect of gifts, etc. received upto Rs. 25,000 in a year from non-relatives. However, gifts received on the occasion of marriage would be exempted without any upper limit. The gift from relatives can be received of any quantum. However, these provisions apply only with reference to gift by cash, cheque or any other mode of payment like gift cheques and travellers cheques. Hence, gift by way of jewellery, property, etc. even from non-relatives can be received without tax.

However, in order to avoid hardships in genuine cases; it is also proposed to exclude certain sums from the scope of the new definition of income under Section 2(24). The sums which shall not be included in the income are:

(a) the sum received by, or credited in the account of (i) any individual from a relative out of natural love and affection, or (ii) any individual or Hindu undivided family under a Will or by way of inheritance, or (iii) any employee or the dependent of the deceased employee from an employer, by way of bonus, gratuity or pension or insurance or any such other sum solely in recognition of the services rendered by the employee, or

(b) any sum received in contemplation of death of an individual or karta or member of a Hindu undivided family, or

(c) any income referred to in Section 10 of the Income Tax Act or any other income which is exempt or not included in the total income under the Act or

(d) any sum received on account of transfers referred to in Section 47 under Income Tax Act. The expression "relative" for the purpose of this provision would be:

   (i)   spouse of the individual.

   (ii)   brother or sister of the individual,

   (iii)   brother or sister of the spouse of the individual,

   (iv)   brother or sister of either of the parents of the individual,

   (v)   any lineal ascendant or descendant of the individual,

   (vi)   any lineal ascendant or descendant of the spouse of the individual, and

   (vii)   spouse of a person referred to in items (ii) to (vi) mentioned above.

On and from F.Y. 2006-07 relevant to the A.Y. 2007-08 the aggregate value of Rs. 50,000 will be exempted from the purview of being taxed as Income from other sources. Moreover, the sum of money received from local authority, or any fund or foundation or university or hospital or other medical institution as mentioned in Section 10(23C) or the trust or institution registered under Section 12AA would be exempted without any upper limit.

This means that if any gift is received, say from a Charity Trust by a meritorious student for higher studies, say of Rs. 4 lakh, then such amount would be exempted from being taxed as income as per Section 56. Similarly, if any help is received from some Trust, etc. for medical treatment, say of Rs. 2 lakh then also it would be tax exempt. However, this benefit would not be available on grant for education or medical help if received from an institution from abroad because the same is not covered in the exemption clause as the exemption only is for Trusts or Institutions mentioned in Section 10 (23C) or Section 12AA of the Income Tax Act, 1961.

The above mentioned provisions would also be applicable to gifts made by an NRI to a non-relative Indian.

12. Conclusion

If the precautions as outlined in the preceding paragraphs are taken, then the income of the gifts would not be clubbed with the income of the donor but would be liable to income tax as well as wealth tax separately. Thus, where a non-resident Indian is interested in having a separate file of income tax for his wife he should see that his wife does not receive any gift from himself as well from his father and mother. Barring these three persons, the married woman may receive the gift of money or assets from any other relations like major son, brother, sister, her father, mother, etc., or the brother of her husband or sister-in-law of her husband, etc. If these precautions are taken, there would not be clubbing of income or wealth in respect of gifts made by the close relations of the non-resident. Likewise, care has to be taken to see that the non-resident Indian does not convert his self-acquired property into HUF. In the same way he should not make a partial partition of HUF.

CHAPTER 4

The incomes of an NRI completely exempt from income tax

1. Introduction

We have seen in the earlier chapters that a non-resident Indian is liable to income tax in India only on the Indian income. Thus, he is not liable to pay any income tax in India on foreign income. Further, even Indian income in the generality of cases is totally exempt from income tax up to Rs. 1,00,000 for the A.Y. 2006-07 and A.Y. 2007-08. The exemption limit is raised to Rs. 1,10,000 from the A.Y. 2008-2009. For resident women tax payers the exemption limit from the A.Y. 2008-2009 is Rs. 1,45,000 while for resident senior citizens it is Rs. 1,95,000. This higher exemption limit is not available for non-resident Indian women and senior citizens. However, this taxable income or total income is computed after excluding all items of income which are completely exempt from income tax. Similarly, there are certain other tax concessions which are in respect of some items which are allowed to be deducted from the gross total income in computing the taxable income. These deductions are described in detail in Chapter 8. Here in this chapter we discussed the most significant items of income which from a practical point of view enjoy total exemption from income tax and are not to be included in the total income for any purposes whatsoever. There are many items of total exemptions which are specially available to a non-resident Indian while there are certain other items which are available to residents and non-residents alike. Further, there are certain items of income which are included in the total income but a concession is given in respect of such items by way of rebate. Such items are known as partial exemptions.

2. Interest on Non-resident (External) Account is fully exempt from income tax

Under the provisions of Section 10(4)(ii) of the Income Tax Act interest on money standing to credit of a person resident outside India or any person who has been permitted by the Reserve Bank of India to maintain the N.R. (External) A/C in a Non-resident (External) Account in any bank in India in accordance with the Foreign Exchange Regulation Act 1973 and now under the Foreign Exchange Management Act, 1999 (regarding FEMA), and any rules made thereunder is completely exempt from income tax. The government had planned to withdraw the exemption in respect of interest income from NRE account w.e.f. 1-4-2005. However, as a result of an amendment introduced by the Finance Act, 2005 the government has withdrawn the proposal to bring it to tax. Hence, as the law stands today the entire income from NRE account and FCNR accounts earned by NRIs will be fully exempted from income-tax. For the purposes of this provision the expression "person resident outside India" is to be distinguished from a non-resident. The expression "person resident outside India" is defined in Section 2(w) of the Foreign Exchange Management Act 1999, as a person who is not resident in India.

Section 2(v) of the Foreign Exchange Management Act 1999, defines the term "person resident in India". According to this definition a "person resident in India" means:

(i) a person residing in India for more than one hundred and eighty-two days during the course of the preceding financial year but does not include—

(A) a person who has gone out of India or who stays outside India, in either case—

(a) for or on taking up employment outside India, or

(b) for carrying on outside India a business or vocation outside India, or

(c) for any other purpose, in such circumstances as would indicate his intention to stay outside India for an uncertain period.

(B) a person who has come to or stays in India, in either case, otherwise than—

(a) for or on taking up employment in India, or

(b) for carrying on India a business or vocation in India, or

(c) for any other purpose, in such circumstances as would indicate his intention to stay in India for an uncertain period.

(ii) any person or body corporate registered or incorporated in India.

(iii) an office, branch or agency in India owned or controlled by a person resident outside India.

(iv) an office, branch or agency outside India owned or controlled by a person resident in India.

Non-resident Indians

Non-resident Indians generally fall under the following broad categories:

(a) Indian citizens who stay abroad for employment or for carrying on business or vocation or any other purpose in circumstances indicating an indefinite period of stay outside India.

(b) Indian citizens working abroad on assignments with foreign governments/government agencies or international/regional agencies like the United Nations (including its affiliates), International Monetary Fund (IMF), World Bank (IBRD), etc.

(c) Officials of the Central and State governments and public sector undertakings deputed abroad on temporary assignments or posted to their offices (including Indian Diplomatic Missions) abroad.

The non-resident Indian becomes resident of India only when he comes back to the country for employment or for carrying on in India any business or vocation or for any other purpose indicating an indefinite period of stay in India. He is not regarded as a person resident in India during his short visits to India, say, for holidays, business visits, etc. Indian citizens who take up jobs on completion of their higher studies abroad are regarded as non-residents only from the time they take up jobs abroad.

It should be noted carefully that this exemption is given not to a non-resident as understood under the Income Tax Act but to a person resident outside India. From a practical point of view and in most of the cases a person resident outside India under the fema and a non-resident person as per the Income Tax Act would be the same. However, in certain cases a person may be resident outside India as per fema but he may not be non-resident in India as per I.T. Act. Likewise, a person may be non-resident in India but he may not be a person resident outside India. This distinction should be carefully followed by a non-resident Indian. However, from practical point of view a non-resident Indian who is generally staying outside India, is regarded as a person resident outside India and is entitled to open a Non-resident (External) Account. Where such an account can be opened in the name of a non-resident Indian because he is regarded as a person resident outside India he would be entitled to this exemption in such a manner that the entire amount of interest on money standing to his Non-resident (External) Account would be completely exempt from income tax. This can be explained by means of an example given below:

Illustration No. 27

A, a non-resident Indian, is regarded as a "person resident outside India" for the purposes of FEMA. He transfers a certain amount of money from the United States of America in US$ equivalent to Rs. 15,00,000 to the Bank of India, New Delhi. He earns interest of Rs. 65,000 on such account during the relevant previous year. His only other income in India is by way of income from house property amounting to Rs. 47,000. A will not be liable to any income tax in India on the sum of Rs. 65,000. Further, his only other taxable income in India amounting to Rs. 47,000 being below the taxable limit of Rs. 1,10,000 is also not liable to any income tax in India. Thus, A is not liable to any income tax in India in respect of the above income for the previous year 2007-2008 (A.Y. 2008-2009.)

---

3. Interest on NSCs is completely exempt from income tax under section 10(4B)

A citizen of India or a person of Indian origin who is a non-resident is not liable to any income tax in India on any income from interest on such savings certificates issued before the 1st day of June, 2002 by the Central Government which may be specified by notification in the Official Gazette. Of course, it is necessary that the non-resident should have subscribed to such certificates in convertible foreign exchange remitted from a country outside India in accordance with the provisions of the Foreign Exchange Management Act 1999, and any rules made thereunder. For the purpose of this clause a person shall be deemed to be of Indian origin if he or either of his parents or any of his grand parents was born in India. Convertible foreign exchange for the purpose of this clause means foreign exchange which is for the time being treated by the Reserve Bank of India as convertible foreign exchange for the purposes of the Foreign Exchange Management Act 1999, and any rules made thereunder.

National Savings Certificates (VI and VII Series) which enjoy a higher rate of interest for non-residents are such certificates which have been so notified under FERA. Hence, interest earned on 6 year National Savings Certificates (VI and VII Series) would be completely exempt from income tax in the case of non-resident Indians.

4. Remuneration of non-citizens is exempt from income tax

The exemptions as described in topic 2 and topic 3 are available to non-resident Indians. There are certain exemptions which are available only to non-citizens of India. Thus, a non-resident who is not a citizen of India even though he may be of Indian origin would also be entitled to such exemptions as are given in Section 10(6) of the Income Tax Act. Some of the important exemptions are described below:

(i) The remuneration received by an individual, who is not a citizen of India as an official of an embassy, etc. is free from income tax, provided that his country offers the exemptions to Indians similarly employed there. These exemptions are under clause (ii) of Section 10(6).

(ii) The remuneration received by a non-citizen as an employee of a foreign enterprise for services rendered by him during his stay in India, provided the foreign enterprise is not engaged in any trade or business in India and his stay does not exceed 90 days in such previous year, is not chargeable under the Income Tax Act. Such remuneration is totally exempt under Section 10(6)(vi). Certain other types of remuneration are also exempt under Section 10(6).

5. Other fully exempted incomes

There are several items of income which are completely exempt from income tax in the case of a non-resident Indian in the same manner as such incomes enjoy full exemption from income tax in the case of resident Indians. Some of the more significant exemptions from a practical point of view are discussed below.

(a) Agricultural Income

Under the provisions of Section 10(1) agricultural income is completely exempt from income tax. Hence, a very good method of tax planning for a non-resident Indian is to have agricultural income in India. For this purpose it would be necessary to know the meaning of "agricultural income". Section 2(1A) of the Income Tax Act defines the expression "agricultural income". In short, agricultural income means any rent or revenue derived from land which is situated in India and which is used for agricultural purposes. Besides, any income derived from such land by agriculture or by the performance of some agricultural process ordinarily employed by the cultivator, etc. to take the produce to the market. This is also regarded as agricultural income. Likewise, any income derived from any building owned and occupied by the receiver of the rent or revenue of any such land used for agricultural purposes or occupation by the cultivator or the receiver of rent-in-kind subject to the condition that the building is on or in the vicinity of the land and is used as a dwelling house or as a store house or other out-building is also exempt from income tax as agricultural income. Where a non-resident Indian has taxable income in India and also agricultural income, the agricultural income is completely exempt from income tax but is, however, added to the other taxable income for the purposes of finding out income tax on taxable Indian income. Thus, a slightly higher income tax would be payable by a non-resident Indian who has taxable income in India and also income from agriculture. Where a non-resident has no taxable income in India, the entire amount of agricultural income, without any limit, is completely exempt from income tax.

(b) Certain interest payments

Interest on P.P.F. a/c is fully exempt under Section 10 (ii) of the I.T. Act. Interest on 15-year Annuity Certificates, on treasury savings, deposit certificates, Post Office Cash Certificates, Post Office National Savings Certificates, National Plan Certificates, 12-year National Plan Savings Certificates and other notified certificates, as well as interest on Post Office Saving Bank Account interest on 8%, 8½, 9% or 10% Relief Bonds received by an individual or a Hindu Undivided Family or NRI Bonds or Bonds of a local authority as may be notified is completely exempt from income tax under different clauses of Section 10(15) of the Income Tax Act in the case of non-resident Indians as it is available for other residents as well. As per Notification No.S.O. 653(E) dated 31st August, 1992 [198 ITR 174(st.)], the Central Government has specified that interest on the deposits in the Non-Resident (Non-repatriable) Rupee Deposit Scheme accruing to non-residents only will be fully exempt from income tax under Section 10(15)(i) of the I.T. Act, 1961. Under Section 10(15)(i) interest on

Resurgent India Bonds would be completely exempt from income tax as per Notification No.844 (E) dated 21.1.1998.

Under the provisions of Section 10(15)(iv)(h), interest on 10.5% Tax-Free Konkan Railway Bonds of the 6th Series would be fully exempt from income tax vide Notification No.743 (E) dated 1.9.1998.

Section 10(15) is reproduced below:

10(15) (i) income by way of interest, premium on redemption or other payment on such securities bonds, annuity certificates savings certificates other certificates, issued by the Central Government and deposits as the Central Government may, by notification in the Official Gazette, specify in this behalf, subject to such conditions and limits as may be specified in the said notification;

(iib) in the case of an individual or a Hindu undivided family, interest on such Capital Investment Bonds as the Central Government may, by notification in the Official Gazette, specify in this behalf before 1-6-2002;

(iic) in the case of an individual or a Hindu undivided family, interest on such Relief Bonds as the Central Government may, by notification in the Official Gazette, specify in this behalf;

(iid) interest on such bonds, as the Central Government may, by notification in the Official Gazette, specify, arising to—

(a) a non-resident Indian, being an individual owning the bonds; or

(b) any individual owning the bonds by virtue of being a nominee or survivor of the non-resident Indian ; or

(c) any individual to whom the bonds have been gifted by the non-resident Indian:

Provided that the aforesaid bonds are purchased by a non-resident Indian in foreign exchange and the interest and principal received in respect of such bonds, whether on their maturity or otherwise, is not allowable to be taken out of India:

Provided further that where an individual, who is a non-resident Indian in any previous year in which the bonds are acquired, becomes a resident in India in any subsequent year, the provisions of this sub-clause shall continue to apply in relation to such individual:

Provided also that in a case where the bonds are encashed in a previous year prior to their maturity by an individual who is so entitled, the provisions of this sub-clause shall not apply to such individual in relation to the assessment year relevant to such previous year.

Provided also that the central government shall not specify, for the purposes of this sub-clause, such bonds on or after the 1st day of June, 2002.

Explanation.—For the purposes of this sub-clause, the expression "non-resident Indian" shall have the meaning assigned to it in clause (e) of Section 115C;]

(iii) interest on securities held by the Issue Department of the Central Bank of Ceylon constituted under the Ceylon Monetary Law Act, 1949;

(iiia) interest payable to any bank incorporated in a country outside India and authorised to perform central banking functions in that country on any deposits made by it, with the approval of the Reserve Bank of India, with any scheduled bank.

Explanation.—For the purposes of this sub-clause, "scheduled bank" shall have the meaning assigned to it in [clause (ii) of the *Explanation* to clause (viia) of sub-section (1) of Section 36];

(iv) interest payable—

(a) by Government or a local authority on moneys borrowed by it before 1.6.2001 from, or debts owed by it before 1.6.2001 to, sources outside India;

(b) by an industrial undertaking in India on moneys borrowed by it under a loan agreement entered into before 1.6.2001 with any such financial institution in a foreign country as may be approved in this behalf by the Central Government by general or special order;

(c) by an industrial undertaking in India on any moneys borrowed or debt incurred by it before 1.6.2001 in a foreign country in respect of the purchase outside India of raw materials or components or capital plant and machinery, to the extent to which such interest does not exceed the amount of interest calculated at the rate approved by the Central Government in this behalf, having regard to the terms of the loan or debt and its repayment.

Explanation.—For the purposes of this item, "purchase of capital plant and machinery" includes the purchase of such capital plant and machinery under a hire-purchase agreement or a lease agreement with an option to purchase such plant and machinery;

(d) by Industrial Finance Corporation of India established by the Industrial Finance Corporation Act, 1948 (15 of 1948), or the Industrial Development Bank of India established under the Industrial Development Bank of India Act, 1964 (18 of 1964), or the Export-

Import Bank of India established under the Export-Import Bank of India Act, 1981 (28 of 1981), or the National Housing Bank established under Section 3 of the National Housing Bank Act, 1987 (53 of 1987), or the Small Industries Development Bank of India established under Section 3 of the Small Industries Development Bank of India Act, 1989 (39 of 1989), or the Industrial Credit and Investment Corporation of India [a company formed and registered under the Indian Companies Act, 1913 (7 of 1913)], on any moneys borrowed by it before 1.6.2001 from sources outside India, to the extent to which such interest does not exceed the amount of interest calculated at the rate approved by the Central Government in this behalf, having regard to the terms of the loan and its repayment;

(e) by any other financial institution established in India or a banking company to which the Banking Regulation Act, 1949 (10 of 1949), applies (including any bank or banking institution referred to in Section 51 of that Act), on any moneys borrowed by it from sources outside India under a loan agreement approved by the Central Government where the moneys are borrowed either for the purpose of advancing loans to industrial undertakings in India for purchase outside India of raw materials or capital plant and machinery or for the purpose of importing any goods which the Central Government may consider necessary to import in the public interest, to the extent to which such interest does not exceed the amount of interest calculated at the rate approved by the Central Government in this behalf, having regard to the terms of the loan and its repayment;

(f) by an industrial undertaking in India on any moneys borrowed by it in foreign currency from sources outside India under a loan agreement approved by the Central Government having regard to the need for industrial development in India, to the extent to which such interest does not exceed the amount of interest calculated at the rate approved by the Central Government before 1.6.2001 in this behalf, having regard to the terms of the loan and its repayment;

(fa) by a scheduled bank to a non-resident or to a person who is not ordinarily resident within the meaning of sub-section (6) of Section 6] on deposits in foreign currency where the acceptance of such deposits by the bank is approved by the Reserve Bank of India.

Explanation.—For the purposes of this item, the expression "scheduled bank" means the State Bank of India constituted under the State Bank of India Act, 1955, a subsidiary bank as defined in the State Bank of India (Subsidiary Banks) Act, 1959, a corresponding new bank constituted under Section 3 of the Banking Companies (Acquisition and Transfer of Undertakings) Act, 1970, or under Section 3 of the Banking Companies (Acquisition and Transfer of Undertakings), Act, 1980, or any other bank being a bank included in the Second Schedule to the Reserve Bank of India Act, 1934, but does not include a co-operative bank;

This has been substituted by the Finance Act, 2007 from the A.Y. 2007-2008.

(g) by a public company formed and registered in India with the main object of carrying on the business of providing long-term finance for construction or purchase of houses in India for residential purposes, being a company eligible for deduction under clause (viii) of sub-section (1) of Section 36 on any moneys borrowed by it in foreign currency from sources outside India under a loan agreement approved by the Central Government before 1-6-2003 to the extent to which such interest does not exceed the amount of interest calculated at the rate approved by the Central Government in this behalf, having regard to the terms of the loan and its repayment.

Explanation.—For the purposes of item (f), (fa) & (g) the expression "foreign currency" shall have the meaning assigned to it in the Foreign Exchange Regulation Act, 1973;

(h) by any public sector company in respect of such bonds or debentures and subject to such conditions, including the condition that the holder of such bonds or debentures registers his name and the holding with that company, as the Central Government may, by notification in the Official Gazette, specify in this behalf;

(i) by Government on deposits made by an employee of the Central Government or a State Government or a public sector company, in accordance with such scheme as the Central Government may, by notification in the Official Gazette, frame in this behalf, out of the moneys due to him on account of his retirement, whether on superannuation or otherwise.

Explanation 1.—For the purposes of this sub-clause, the expression "industrial undertaking" means any undertaking which is engaged in—

(a) the manufacture or processing of goods; or

(aa) the manufacture of computer software or recording of programme on any disc, tape, perforated media or other information device; or

(b) the business of generation or distribution of electricity or any other form of power; or

(ba) the business of providing telecommunication services; or]

(c) mining; or

(d) the construction of ships; or

(e) the operation of ships or aircrafts or construction or operation of rail systems;

Explanation 1A—For the purposes of this sub-clause, the expression "interest" shall not include interest paid on delayed payment of loan or on default if it is in excess of 2% p.a. over the rate of interest payable in terms of such loan.

Explanation 2.—For the purposes of this clause, the expression "interest" includes hedging transaction charges on account of currency fluctuation;

(v) interest on—

(a) securities held by the Welfare Commissioner, Bhopal Gas Victims, Bhopal, in the Reserve Bank's SGL Account No. SL/DH 048;

(b) deposits for the benefit of the victims of the Bhopal gas leak disaster held in such account, with the Reserve Bank of India or with a public sector bank, as the Central Government may, by notification in the Official Gazette, specify, whether prospectively or retrospectively but in no case earlier than the 1st day of April, 1994 in this behalf.

Explanation.—For the purposes of this sub-clause, the expression "public sector bank" shall have the meaning assigned to it in the Explanation to clause (23D);

(vi) interest on Gold Deposit Bonds issued under the Gold Deposit Scheme, 1999 notified by the Central Government;

(vii) interest on bonds—

(a) issued by a local authority or by a State Pooled Finance Entity; and

(b) specified by the Central Government by notification in the Official Gazette.

Explanation.—For the purposes of this sub-clause, the expression "State Pooled Finance Entity" shall mean such entity which is set up in accordance with the guidelines;

This has been substituted by the Finance Act, 2007 from the A.Y. 2008-2009.

(c) Scholarships

Under Section 10(16) scholarships granted to meet the cost of education are completely exempt from income tax.

(d) Dividends on shares and income from units, etc.

The dividend income from shares of companies as also the income from all types of Mutual Funds is fully exempt from tax. The long-term capital gains on shares and mutual funds on which securities transaction tax has been paid would be exempt from tax from 1.10.2004.

(e) Income of certain venture capital undertakings — Section 10 (23FB).

The Finance Act, 2007 has, with effect from the A.Y. 2008-2009 provided a new definition of venture capital undertaking, where the investment of a Venture Capital Company or Venture Capital Fund would be exempt from tax. Thus, "venture capital undertaking" means such domestic company whose shares are not listed in a recognized stock exchange in India and which is engaged in the:

I. business of:
   (A) Nanotechnology
   (B) Information technology relating to hardware and software development;
   (C) Seed research and development;
   (D) Bio-technology;
   (E) Research and development of new chemical entities in the pharmaceutical sector;
   (F) Production of bio-fuels; or
   (G) Building and operating composite hotel-cum-convention centre with seating capacity of more than three thousand; or
   (H) Developing or operating and maintaining or developing, operation and maintaining any infrastructure facility as defined in Section 80 IA(4).

II. Dairy or poultry industry.

6. NRI Bonds (Second Series) had attractive tax exemptions

NRI Bonds (Second Series – 7 years) could be gifted to any individual of Indian nationality or origin (resident or non-resident), or to a charitable trust recognised under the Income Tax Act.

7. India Development Bonds offered attractive tax exemptions

In February 1992 the SBI issued India Development Bonds. These enjoyed total exemption on the interest income and they could be gifted without any gift tax liability. Further, they enjoyed total freedom from enquiry as to the source of the money under all direct tax laws and FERA.

8. Exemption on interest in foreign currency deposits in Indian banks for non-residents and not ordinarily residents

With effect from assessment year 1993-94, interest on foreign currency deposits in banks in India, allowed now by the RBI, are fully exempt from income tax under Section 10(15)(iv)(fa) only in the case of non-residents and not-ordinarily resident individuals and Hindu Undivided Families. Thus, residents will not get this exemption.

9. Resurgent India Bonds (RIB)

The SBI offered Resurgent India Bonds to NRIs from August 5, 1998 upto August 24, 1998. These bonds were issued to individual NRIs, OCBs & banks on behalf of NRIs & OCBs. Their tenure was 5 years. The currencies were US Dollar, Pond Sterling & Deutsche Mark. Interest rate was 7.75% p.a. on USD, 8% p.a on GBP & 6.25% p.a. on DEM. Payment of interest is half yearly or cumulative. Principal and interest is fully repatriable to NRIs. Interest is exempt from I.T. & the Bonds are exempt from W.T. These benefits are also available to transferee and donee holders. These are transferable between NRIs/OCBs by endorsement and delivery. Premature encashment is permitted only in non-repatriable rupees without penalty. Loans in rupees to holders and third parties is available against collateral security of the Bonds. The collection was US $ 4.16 billions.

10. Insurance Policy — Maturity proceeds

Amount received on maturity of insurance policy is exempt. The Finance Act, 2003 w.e.f. the A.Y. 2004-2005 provides that exemption under Section 10(10D) shall not be allowed on any sum received under an insurance policy issued on or after 1-4-2003 in respect of which the premium payable for any of the years during the term of the policy exceeds 20% of the actual capital sum assured. However, on death before maturity of the policy these provisions will not apply.

11. Income in Special Economic Zones, 100% EOUs etc.

From a practical point of view, over 90% of the non-resident Indians will be able to compute their total income as well as their income tax liability in India by having a knowledge of the different provisions of the Income Tax Act, 1961, as explained in Chapter 8 as also in the previous ones. The NRIs should, therefore, remember these provisions well. They should further remember that they can now enjoy a ten-year tax holiday upto the A.Y. 2009-10 in respect of the profits of new industrial undertakings set up in a Free Trade Zone, etc. under Section 10A of the Income Tax Act. Likewise, they can enjoy a 10-year tax holiday upto the A.Y. 2009-10 in respect of the profits of 100% Export Oriented Units under Section 10B of the Income Tax Act. However, 10% of the income of units in FTZ and EOU would be subjected to tax for A.Y. 2003-2004 only. New industrial undertakings set up in Special Economic Zones on or after 1.4.2002 will be eligible to 100% deduction for five years. For the next two assessment years, however, exemption would be only to the extent of 50% of their profits. A change in the ownership of the industrial undertaking would debar it from getting the exemption. However, when the change is from a proprietary or partnership firm to a company on succession, then the restriction will not apply if not less than 51% voting power is kept with the earlier partners or proprietor. The latter exemption is different from the previous one inasmuch as "manufacturing" by a 100% Export Oriented Undertaking would include any process or assembly or recording of programmes on any disc, tape, perforated media or other information storage device. Likewise, "produce" in relation to any article or thing would include production of computer programmes and export of software for the purposes of exemption under Section 10B, which is not covered under Section 10A.

The Finance Act, 2003 has w.e.f. the A.Y. 2004-2005 amended Section 10A and Section 10B to provide that where an undertaking of an Indian company is transferred to another company under a scheme of amalgamation or demerger, the deduction would be allowed in the hands of the amalgamated or the resultant company.

The benefit of deduction under Section 10A and 10B has been extended to the business of cutting and polishing of precious and semi-precious stones from the A.Y. 2004-2005.

As per the Finance Act, 2005 a sun set clause has been inserted to provide that no deduction to an undertaking set up in a Special

Economic Zone which begins to manufacture or produce articles or things or computer software after 31.3.2009 in a Special Economic Zone would be allowed as a tax holiday. It is also provided that such undertakings should file income tax return in time to avail of the benefit.

The Taxation Laws (Amendment) Act, 2005 provides that if deduction was not granted u/s 10A, 10B or 10C due to non receipt of convertible foreign exchange which is received later on, then the deduction under the above sections can be granted within four years from the end of the previous year in which the amount is brought in India.

From the A.Y. 2006-07, under Section 10AA newly established units in Special Economic Zones would get a 100% tax holiday for five consecutive assessment years and a 50% tax holiday for the next further five assessment years in respect of export profits with a further tax benefit of 50% tax holiday for the next 5 years on the fulfilment of some conditions.

12. Exemption of wood handicraft export profits — Section 10BA

On and from the financial year 2003-04 (i.e., A.Y. 2004-2005) a special exemption under Section 10BA is available to all those exporters who are located in free trade zone or who are working in an undertaking established as a 100% export-oriented undertaking in respect of hand made articles or things of artistic value which requires the use of wood as the main raw material. Such undertakings should employ 20 or more workers. The deduction would not be allowed from the assessment year beginning on the first day of April, 2010.

CHAPTER 5

Capital gains of an NRI could be completely exempt from income tax

1. What is capital gain?

An NRI, like a resident person is liable to income tax on capital gain. However, there are various exemptions available to different types of capital gains. An NRI could take advantage of the various exemptions available under the Income Tax Act, 1961 and thus, save income tax Hence, the important provisions concerning the capital gains and the important exemptions along with the concept of Cost Inflation Index are discussed in relevant details in this chapter. Unnecessary technical provisions as also provisions concerning capital gains in special cases and the very special types of exemptions not concerning nearly 99% of the NRIs are not discussed in this chapter. It is provided in Section 45 (1) that tax is payable by an assessee under the head "Capital Gains" in respect of any profits arising from the transfer, i.e. sale, exchange, relinquishment of a capital asset, etc. Such profits or capital gains would be deemed to be income of the previous year in which the sale, etc. took place. It is also provided by Section 45(1) that profits and gains arising from the receipt of an insurance claim on account of destruction or damage of a capital asset as a result of flood, typhoon, hurricane, cyclone, earthquake or other convulsion of nature, or riot or civil disobedience or accidental fire or explosion, or action by an enemy, etc. would be deemed to be capital gains and would be taxed in the year of receipt. Besides the actual capital gains the Income Tax Act also treats certain gains as deemed capital gains. For example, on conversion of a capital asset into stock-in-trade, there is a provision for charging income tax on the deemed capital gains, Likewise, on the transfer of firm's assets to partners and vice-versa, there is a provision of deemed capital gains. Further, in case of any enhanced compensation on compulsory acquisition of property received subsequently, the compensation so received is charged to tax as capital gains of the year in which such amount is received. In case of enhanced compensation received, the cost of acquisition and improvement is taken to be Nil. If due to the death of the original transferor or for any other reason, enhanced compensation is received by any other person, it is deemed to be the income of the recipient.

A loss under the head "Capital gains" can be carried forward for 8 assessment years for set off against "Capital gains" only. Also *see* Chapter 2, topic 7.

2. Meaning of "capital asset"

The expression "Capital Asset" as per Section 2(14) of the I.T. Act means property of any kind held by an assessee, whether or not connected with his business or profession. However, it does not include the following:

(i) Any stock-in-trade, consumable stores or raw materials held for the purposes of his business or profession;

(ii) Personal effects (i.e., movable property like wearing apparel, furniture, etc. but excluding jewellery, paintings, drawings, works of art, etc.);

(iii) Agricultural land in India (except certain types of urban land);

(iv) 6-1/2% Gold Bonds 1977 or the National Defence Gold Bond, 1980, issued by the Central Government;

(v) Special Bearer Bonds, 1991, issued by the Central Government;

(vi) Gold Deposit Bonds, 1999.

Agricultural land situated within the limits of any municipality or cantonment board having population of 10,000 or more according to the latest census for which the figures have been published before the 1st day of the previous year is not excluded. Further, agricultural land situated in areas lying within a distance of 8 k.m. from the local limits of such municipalities or cantonment boards will also be covered if such areas are so notified by the Government.

3. Short-term and long-term capital gains

It is very important for an NRI to understand the distinction between the expression "Short-term and Long-term Capital Gains". This is because an NRI may become liable to income tax without being able to avail himself of any exemption if the capital gain is a short-term one. In respect of long-term capital gains, however, various exemptions are available. Hence, it is very necessary for an NRI to know the distinction between long-term capital gains and short-term capital gains. Long-term capital gain means capital gain arising from the transfer of a long-term capital asset. Short-term capital gain means capital gain arising from the transfer of a short-term capital asset. Hence, it is necessary to know the meaning of the expression "Short-term capital asset". As per Section 2(42A), "Short-term capital asset" means a capital asset held by an assessee for not more than 36 months immediately preceding the date of its transfer. However, in the case of a share, units of UTI & Mutual Funds and securities traded in the recognised stock exchanges, it means a capital asset held for not more than 12 months, The cost of rights entitlement in the hands of the original share-holder is deemed to be Nil. Where the rights renouncee acquires the rights share, the cost of the rights share will be equal to the cost incurred by him for purchasing the rights entitlement plus the price paid by him to the company for acquiring the rights share. The period of holding of the rights entitlement will be reckoned from the date of offer made by the company to the date of renouncement. Where a capital asset becomes the property of the assessee by way of gift or Will, etc., the period for which the asset was held by the previous owner would also be included. A capital asset which is not a short-term capital asset is known as a long-term capital asset as per Section (29A). The rate of income tax on long-term capital gains is generally 20% for individuals, HUFs, companies, and firms & AOPs. In respect of long-term capital gains arising from listed securities the rate of tax is 10% without applying the Cost Inflation Index.

A short-term capital gain is taxable to the hands of the assessee like any other income. However, certain deductions under Section 48 as given in topic 6 and other exemptions as mentioned in topic 5 are allowed in respect of long-term capital gains. Hence, the distinction between long-term capital gains and short-term capital gains is to be understood carefully. Likewise, long-term capital losses and short-term capital losses have to be distinguished.

4. Exemption of long-term capital gains regarding residential house property (Section 54)

An NRI is permitted to invest without any formal permission of RBI in a residential house property in India. The residential house property may be self-occupied or a tenanted one. If there is a long-term capital gain on the sale of a residential house property, then it is provided in

Section 54 that if the long-term capital gain is fully invested in the purchase of a residential house property, within one year before or two years after the transfer of the first house property, the entire long-term capital gains would be fully exempt from income tax. Further, this exemption is also available if the entire long-term capital gain is invested in the construction of a new house property in three years from the date of the transfer. However, if the long-term capital gain exceeds the cost of the new property so acquired, the excess would be taxable.

5. Exemption of long-term capital gains from any capital asset on investment in house property (Section 54F)

It is also provided by Section 54F that where any long-term capital gain arises from the transfer of any long-term capital asset (other than a residential house) and the assessee, being an individual or a Hindu Undivided family, purchases within a year before or two years after the date on which the transfer took place or constructs within a period of three years from the transfer, a residential house, the capital gain arising from the transfer will be treated in a concessional manner, i.e. the entire capital gain arising from the transfer would be exempt from income-tax if the cost of the house that has been purchased or constructed is not less than the net consideration in respect of the capital asset so transferred. If, however, the cost of the newly acquired house is less than the net consideration in respect of the asset transferred, the exemption from long-term capital gains will be granted proportionately on the basis of investment of net sale consideration either for purchase or construction of a residential house. Even if the assessee owns not more than one residential house as on the date of transfer of the original asset, he would be eligible to this exemption from the assessment year 2001-2002. However, this concession will not be available where the assessee owns on the date of the transfer of the original asset more than one residential house, or purchases within the period of one year after such date, or constructs within a period of three years after such date, any other residential house. In such cases, the exemption allowed would stand forfeited. Another important condition which should be noted by an NRI is that if he transfers the newly acquired residential house within three years of its purchase or construction, then the amount of capital gain arising from the transfer of the original asset which was not charged to tax would be deemed to be the income of the year in which the new asset is transferred. In such a case the income would be charged to tax under the head "Capital gains". This provision is also applicable for the exemption of long-term capital gains under Section 54 as described in topic 4 above.

6. Exemption of long-term capital gains on investment in bonds of NHAI & REC

With effect from the A.Y. 2001-2002, a new Section 54EC was inserted in the I.T. Act to provide for exemption in respect of long-term capital gains in the hands of any assessee, whether an NRI or a resident assessee. This exemption is in respect of long-term capital gains of any asset which are invested in select bonds, redeemable after a period of three years issued on or after 1 April 2000 by the National Highways Authority of India (NHAI) and on bonds of Rural Electrification Corporation Ltd., etc. The exemption from income tax on long-term capital gains of the NRI would be to the extent of investment not exceeding Rs. 50 lakh in these bonds. These bonds have a lock-in-period of three years. Interest rate is around five and a half per cent per annum. Any transfer or conversion of bonds into money during the lock-in period would make the amount so converted as deemed capital gains to be taxable in the year of transfer or conversion. Similarly, such deemed capital gains would also arise, if any loan or advance is taken on the security of these bonds.

As per the Finance Act, 2006 the Bonds issued only by NHAI and REC would qualify for exemption of long-term capital gains under Section 54EC, as are issued on and after 1.4.2006.

7. Exemption to facilitate the conversion of partnership firm into a company

Full exemption is allowed in respect of capital gains on the conversion of a partnership firm into a company, under Section 47(xiii). Thus, it is provided that where a firm is succeeded by a company in the business carried on by it as a result of which the firm sells or otherwise transfers any capital asset, or intangible assets to the company, the entire capital gains would be exempt from tax provided the following conditions are fulfilled:

(a) All the assets and liabilities of the firm relating to business immediately before the succession become the assets and liabilities of the company;

(b) All the partners of the firm immediately before the succession become the shareholders of the company in the same proportion in which their capital accounts stood in the books of the firm on the date of succession;

(c) The partners of the firm do not receive any consideration or benefit directly or indirectly in any form or manner other than by way of allotment of shares in the company: and

(d) The aggregate of the shareholding in the company of partners of the firm is not less than 50% of the total voting power in the company and their shareholding continues to be as such for a period of five years from the date of succession. This has been extended to a stock exchange converted into a company, as per SEBI approval for de mutualisation or corporatisation where the transaction would not be treated as "transfer" under Section 47(xiiia) from the A.Y. 2004-2005.

8. Exemption from the levy of capital gains tax to facilitate conversion of sole proprietary concern into a company

Likewise, when a sole proprietary concern is succeeded by a company in business carried on by it as a result of which the sole proprietary concern sells or otherwise transfers any capital asset or intangible assets to the company, the entire amount of capital gains would be fully exempt from tax under Section 47(xiv) from the A.Y. 1999-2000. However, the following conditions are to be fulfilled:

(a) All the assets and liabilities of the sole proprietary concern relating to the business immediately before the succession become the assets and liabilities of the company;

(b) The shareholding of the sole proprietor in the company is not less than 50% of the total voting power in the company and his shareholding continues to so remain as such for a period of five years from the date of the succession; and,

(c) The sole proprietor does not receive any consideration or benefit, directly or indirectly, in any form or manner other than by way of allotment of shares in the company.

9. Computation of capital gains in real estate transactions

The Finance Act, 2002 had, with effect from the A.Y. 2003-2004 inserted a new Section 50C in the Income Tax Act, 1961, to make a special provision for determining the full value of consideration in cases of transfer of immovable property. This provided that where the consideration declared to be received or accruing as a result of the transfer of land or building or both is less than the value adopted or assessed by any authority of the State Government for the purpose of payment of stamp duty in respect of such transfer, the value so adopted or assessed would be deemed to be the full value of the consideration, and the capital gains would be computed accordingly under Section 48 of the I.T. Act. It was further provided that where the assessee claims that the value adopted or assessed for stamp duty purposes exceeds the fair market value of the property as on the date of transfer and he has not disputed the value so adopted or assessed in any appeal or revision or reference before any authority or Court, the Assessing Officer may refer the valuation of the relevant asset to a Valuation Officer in accordance with Section 55A of the Income Tax Act. If the fair market value determined by the Valuation Officer is less than the value adopted for stamp duty purposes, the Assessing Officer may take such fair market value to be the full value of consideration. However, if the fair market determined by the Valuation Officer is more than the value adopted or assessed for stamp duty purposes, the Assessing Officer would not adopt such fair market value and would take the full value of consideration to be the value adopted or assessed for stamp duty purposes. It was also provided that if the value adopted or assessed for stamp duty purposes is revised in any appeal, revision or reference, the assessment made would be amended to recompute the capital gains by taking the revised value as the full value of consideration.

10. Other important exemptions regarding capital gains

The following are some of the important exemptions regarding capital gains available to an NRI under different sections of the Income Tax Act:

(1) Gains as a result of distribution of the capital asset of a company in liquidation (Section 46).

(2) Gains arising on the distribution of capital assets on the partition of a Hindu undivided family (Section 47(i)).

(3) Gains arising on the transfer of capital asset under a gift, or will or an irrevocable trust (Section 47(iii)). This is not applicable for

shares received by an employee under ESOP and gifted or transferred under an irrevocable trust.

(4) Gains arising on the transfer by a parent company of its capital assets to a wholly-owned Indian subsidiary company which is resident in India (Section 47(iv)).

(5) Gains as a result of transfer of a capital asset by a 100% subsidiary company to its Indian holding company (Section 47(v)). However, this and Section 47(iv) will not be applicable to the transfer of a capital asset after 29.2.88 as stock-in-trade.

(6) Gains arising out of any transfer of a capital asset by the amalgamating company to the amalgamated Indian company, in a scheme of amalgamation (Section 47(vi)).

(7) Gains arising out of any transfer in a scheme of amalgamation of shares held in an Indian company subject to certain conditions (Section 47(via)).

(8) Gains arising out of any transfer, in a demerger, of a capital asset by the demerged company to the resulting company, if the resulting company is an Indian company (Section 47(vib)).

(9) Gains arising of any transfer in a demerger, of a capital asset, being a share or shares held in an Indian company, by the demerged foreign company to the resulting foreign company, if —
(a) at least seventy-five per cent, of the shareholders of the demerged foreign company continue, to remain shareholders of the resulting foreign company, and (b) such transfer does not attract tax on capital gains in the country, in which the demerged foreign company is incorporated:

Provided that the provisions of Sections 391 to 394 of the Companies Act. 1956 shall not apply in case of demergers referred to in this clause (Section 47(vic)).

(10) Gains arising out of any transfer or issue of shares by the resulting company, in a scheme of demerger to the shareholders of the demerged company if the transfer or issue is made in consideration of demerger of the undertaking (Section 47(vid)).

(11) Gains arising out of any transfer by a shareholder, in a scheme of amalgamation of a capital asset being a share or shares held by him in the amalgamating company, if the transfer is made in consideration of the allotment to him of any share or shares in the amalgamated Indian Company (Section 47(vii)).

(12) Gains arising out of transfer of bonds or shares as referred to in Section 115AC(1) made outside India by a non-resident to another non-resident (Section 47(viia)).

(13) Gains arising from the transfer of a capital asset, being any work of art, archaeological, scientific or art collection, book, manuscript, drawing, painting, photograph or print in cases where such asset is transferred by the assessee to the Government or a University or the National Museum, National Art Gallery. National Archives or any such other notified public museum or institution (Section 47(ix)). In certain cases before the expiry of 8 years from the date of transfer of capital asset under Section 47(iv) or if it is converted into stock-in-trade, the gains would be taxable in the year of first transfer as per Section 47A.

(14) Transfer involved in a scheme for lending of any securities under an agreement or arrangement subject to the guidelines issued by the SEBI in this regard, which the assessee has entered with the borrower of such securities, so that it is not treated as a transfer in order to attract the levy of capital gains tax, as per Section 47(xv).

(15) Capital gains arising from the transfer of an agricultural land which was used by the assessee or a parent of his for agricultural purposes, and invested in the purchase of any other agricultural land for agricultural purposes within the next two years. This would enable the assessee to have complete exemption from income-tax on capital gains if the amount of capital gains is equal to or less than the cost of the new asset, as per Section 54B.

The Finance Act, 2001, had, w.e.f. the A.Y. 2002-2003 provided that the long-term capital gains on transfer of listed securities or units of a mutual fund or the UTI would be exempt from tax to the extent such capital gain is invested in equity shares forming part of an eligible issue made by a public company, and offered for subscription to public. There would be a lock-in-period of one year and if the newly acquired shares are sold or transferred during this period, the capital gains from the original asset would be charged to tax in the year of sale of transfer. Where the cost of the new equity shares has been taken into account for the purposes of this section, a deduction from the amount of income tax with reference to such cost would not be allowed under Section 88. Also see Chapter 4, para 5(e).

11. Cost Inflation Index and computation of capital gains

The following deductions from the value of the consideration for which the sale, etc. is made are allowed in computing the amount of taxable long-term capital gains:

(i) expenditure incurred wholly and exclusively in connection with such transfer; and

(ii) the cost of acquisition of the asset and the cost of any improvement thereon.

In respect of a long-term capital asset acquired before 1 April, 1981, the assessee is allowed the option to substitute its market value on 1 April, 1981 in place of the cost of acquisition. Further, such cost of acquisition is to be substituted by the "Indexed cost of Acquisition" based on the notified Cost Inflation Index for the year of transfer and the year of acquisition or 1 April 1981, whichever is later. However, from A.Y. 1998-99, as per the new 3rd proviso in Section 48, this facility of Cost Inflation Index is not available on bonds and debentures. The notified Cost Inflation Index for the financial years 1981-82 to 2006-2007 is 100, 109, 116, 125, 133, 140, 150, 161, 172, 182, 199, 223, 244, 259, 281, 305, 331, 351, 389, 406, 426, 447, 463, 480, 497 and 519 respectively. Similarly, the cost of improvement can also be indexed by the Cost Inflation Index.

In the case of a capital asset received under a gift or will, etc. the cost to the previous owner is to be considered. The cost of acquisition in case of goodwill, bonus shares, tenancy rights, trade marks, brand names, etc. under Section 55 would be deemed to be nil.

A special facility is allowed to a non-resident. It is provided by the first proviso to Section 48 that in the case of a non-resident assessee, capital gains arising from the transfer of a capital asset being shares in or debentures of Indian companies shall be computed by converting the cost of acquisition, expenditure incurred wholly and exclusively in connection with such transfer and the full value of the consideration received or accruing as a result of the transfer of the capital asset into the same foreign currency as was initially utilised in the purchase of the shares or debentures. The capital gains so computed in such foreign currency, would then be reconverted into Indian currency, so however, that the aforesaid manner of computation of capital gains would be applicable in respect of capital gains accruing or arising from every reinvestment thereafter, in, and sale of, shares in, or debentures of an Indian company.

As mentioned earlier, it is also provided that the provisions of Cost Inflation Index will not be applicable to the NRIs in the above case. Likewise, the advantage of Cost Inflation Index is also not available in respect of computation of long-term capital gains relating to bonds or debentures other than Capital Index Bonds issued by the Government. Under the fourth proviso to Section 48 from the A.Y. 2001-2002, it was provided that where shares, debentures or warrant referred to in the proviso to clause (iii) of Section 47 are transferred under a gift, or will or an irrevocable trust, the market value on the date of such transfer would be deemed to be the full value of consideration received or accruing as a result of transfer for the purposes of Section 48.

12. Reduction of tax rate on long-term capital gains in regard to shares and securities

The normal rate of income tax on long-term capital gains is 20%. As regards an NRI, we have discussed the detailed provisions regarding the tax on capital gains relating to foreign exchange assets in Chapter 7. Sometimes an NRI may have investment in shares and securities, like any other resident person. It was provided in Section 112, from the A.Y. 2000-2001 that the income tax on long-term capital gains will be limited at 10% of the long-term capital gains on shares and securities as defined in Section 2(h) of the Securities Contract (Regulation) Act, 1956 and listed in recognised stock exchanges in India and units of UTI and Mutual Funds, before allowing adjustment of Cost Inflation Index for all assessees.

13. Concessional rate of tax on income from certain global depository receipts

The Finance Act. 1999 had, with effect from the A.Y. 2000-2001, inserted a new Section 115ACA relating to tax on income from Global Depository Receipts (GDR) purchased in foreign currency or capital gains arising from transfer. Thus, it is provided that on the income by way of dividends or long-term capital gains in respect of GDRs of an Indian company purchased by a resident employee of such company in accordance with the notified employee's stock option scheme, the income tax payable would be at the rate of 10%. This concessional rate of 10% would only apply to the income from investment in GDRs of a resident employee of a domestic company engaged in information technology software and information technology services. Of course, no other deduction in respect of such dividend income and long-term capital gains would be allowed in the case of such resident employee.

The first and the second provisos to Section 48(1) would also not apply while computing the long-term capital gains in such a case. The scope of this concession has been widened by the Finance Act, 2001.

14. Tax treatment of capital gain on sale of shares, debentures, etc. received under ESOP

The Finance Act, 2000 had amended the definition of Section 47 relating to transaction not regarded as transfer. It was provided in Section 47 that any transfer of a capital asset under gift or an irrevocable trust is not a transfer and hence not liable to tax on capital gains. The new amendment to this provision by the Finance Act, 2000 provided that this clause would not be applicable to transfer under a gift or an irrevocable trust of the capital asset being shares, debentures or warrant allotted by the company directly or indirectly to its employees under the employees stock option plan or scheme. The effect of this new amendment is that the shares, debentures, etc. received under ESOP would be treated as a transfer when the same are gifted by the employee. Thus, if the employee receives any share or debenture, etc. from his employer without any cost or at a concessional price and makes a gift of such shares, debentures, etc. to some other person, then it will be treated as a transfer and would be subject to tax on capital gains. Section 48 was amended to provide the mode of computation of capital gain in respect of gift, etc. of the shares, debentures, etc. received under ESOP. It was also provided as per amendment by the Finance Act, 2000 that if the shares, debentures, etc. which are received by an employee under employees stock option plan are transferred through gift, etc., then the value on the date of such transfer would be deemed to be the full value of the consideration received or accruing as a result of the transfer for the purposes of this section and thus, there will be a liability to capital gain in the situation where the shares, debentures, etc. received under ESOP are gifted away. This is effective from the A.Y. 2001-2002. The value of ESOP will be liable to FBT for the company. At a later date when the employee sells such shares, etc., received in ESOP and if Capital Gain arises from the transfer of such shares, etc. then from the sale price would be deducted the value of Fringe Benefits which have been taxed in the hands of the employer. The Central Board of Direct Taxes will prescribe the mode of determination of the fair market value. The Fringe Benefit Tax on the entire value on the date of vesting would be payable @ 30% plus surcharge land cesses.

The above position of the Law will be well explained by the way of an example:

Company A Ltd. on 31.1.2007 decides to allot 1000 shares of the face value of Rs. 100 in next 10 years at zero value to an employee. The market value of these shares is also Rs. 100 per share. Now the employee will receive in each of the ten financial years the shares at Nil value. During the Financial Year 2007-2008 on 5 May 2007 the employee receives 100 shares. The market value of shares on 5 May 2007 is Rs. 210. Now, as per the Finance Act, 2007 the employer would be liable to payment of Fringe Benefit Tax during the Financial Year 2007-2008 on Rs. 100 per share being the price as on the date of vesting. As and when the employee sells the shares, then from his sale price would be deducted the sum of Rs. 100 being the amount on which FBT was paid by the employer. Now let us presume that in the seventh year the market value of the share is Rs. 710 but still the FBT in the seventh year when shares are transferred to the employee would be payable on Rs. 100 only being the value on the date of vesting of the shares.

15. Provisions relating to set-off of long-term capital loss and carry forward thereof modified — Sections 70 and 74

The Finance Act, 2002 had, with effect from the A.Y. 2003-2004, amended Section 70 of the I.T. Act, 1961, to provide that while losses from transfer of short-term capital assets can be set off against any capital gains, whether short-term or long-term, losses arising from transfer of long-term capital assets would be allowed to be set off only against long-term capital gains. Through an amendment of Section 74 of the I.T. Act, 1961, it is further provided that a long-term capital loss would be carried forward separately for eight assessment years to be set off only against long-term capital gains. However, a short-term capital loss may be carried forward and set off against any income under the head "Capital gains". Also see Chapter 2, topic 8.

16. Exemption of long-term capital gains on securities and lower tax on short-term capital gains

As a result of insertion of Section 10 (38) by the Finance (No.2) Act, 2004 the income arising from the transfer of a long-term capital asset being equity shares as also units of equity-oriented mutual funds would be exempted from the purview of long-term capital gains.

This exemption is, however, not applicable on capital gains arising on sale of any type of equity share. It is very clearly mentioned that the exemption from tax in respect of such long-term capital gains would be available only when the transaction relating to sale of equity share or units of equity-oriented is entered into on or after 1-10-2004, the date on which Chapter VII of the Finance (No. 2) Act, 2004 came into force. Another condition to avail this exemption is that such transaction is chargeable to Securities Transaction Tax (STT). If a person sells shares of a listed company directly to a friend without routing it through a stock broker, then the benefits of exemption of long-term capital gains on such sale of equity shares would not be available.

Similarly, if the shares of a private limited company are sold after holding them for more than 12 months, then the above mentioned benefits would not be available because such shares are not sold through the stock broker and thus the transaction is not subjected to STT. Therefore, in view of the fact that the shares of a Private Limited Company are not chargeable to STT, the same would not enjoy any tax benefits.

If the sale of units of an equity-oriented fund results into a long-term capital gains, it would also be tax free if the said transaction is chargeable to STT.

It has been clarified that "equity-oriented fund" would mean a fund where the investible funds are invested in equity shares of domestic companies to the extent of more than 65% of total corpus of the fund. Moreover, such a fund should have been set up as a scheme of a mutual fund in terms of Section 23D of the Income-tax Act, 1961. It has also clarified that the percentage of equity share holding of the fund shall be computed as the annual average of its average monthly holding of equity based on opening and closing figures. Thus, where a mutual fund has exposure to equity investment of, say, only 45% to 50%, then the above mentioned benefit would not be available.

As a result of new Section 111A the tax on income arising to all categories of tax payers on transfer of a short-term capital asset being an equity share in a company or unit of an equity-oriented mutual fund would be only 10%.

However, this provision would not be applicable to all transactions of shares and units of equity mutual fund resulting in short-term capital gains but is limited only to:

- Transactions entered on or after 1-10-2004, i.e., the date on which the Chapter VII of the Finance (No. 2) Act, 2004 came into force, and

■ That such transaction is chargeable to STT.

Only when both these conditions are fulfilled is the special 10% tax on such short-term capital gains applicable. It is, therefore, clear that when a short-term capital gain arises on selling equity shares or units of equity fund which does not attract STT, then the concessional rate of income tax of just 10% on short-term capital gains would not be applicable and tax would be payable on the short-term capital gains, like an other income as per applicable slab rates.

It is further provided that in the case of an individual or a Hindu undivided family, being a resident, where the total income as reduced by such short-term capital gains is below the exemption limit, then such short-term capital gains shall be reduced by the amount by which the total income, as so reduced, falls short of the maximum amount which is not chargeable to income-tax and the tax on the balance of such short-term capital gains shall be computed at the rate of 10%. A person having short-term capital gains and other incomes, the deduction under Chapter VIA as well as the tax rebate would be allowed after reducing the said short-term capital gains.

17. Miscellaneous provisions regarding capital gains

As discussed above, the provisions regarding the treatment of capital gains in relation to foreign exchange assets have been discussed in detail in Chapter 7. An NRI, as permitted under FEMA may invest in the immovable property or in shares, securities or units of Mutual Funds, etc. Different provisions relating to the complete exemption from income tax particularly the one under Section 54EC applicable to long-term capital gains upto Rs 50 lakh only in respect of all types of assets would be of special benefit for the NRIs in particular. We have not discussed the provisions regarding the computation of capital gains in the case of slump sales or on the shifting of industrial undertakings or compulsory acquisition of land and building, etc. By remembering the provisions analysed in this chapter, NRIs would be able to save substantial money in respect of income tax on capital gains.

CHAPTER 6

Items completely exempt from wealth tax for an NRI

1. Introduction

We have seen in the earlier chapters that a non-resident Indian is liable to Wealth-tax in India only when his net taxable wealth tax in India exceeds Rs 15 lakhs with effect from the Assessment Year 1993-94 on the valuation date relevant to a particular assessment year. Thus, wealth tax outside India is generally exempt in the case of a non-resident Indian. Further, there are various items of wealth tax which enjoy such exemption because the taxpayer happens to be a non-resident Indian. Further, they are entitled to complete exemption in respect of certain other items of wealth tax like resident Indians. All these exemptions which are practical significance are described in this chapter. The sections referred to in this chapter are of the Wealth Tax Act 1957, unless otherwise specified.

2. Only non-productive wealth is liable to wealth tax from assessment year 1993-94.

The Finance Act 1992 made fundamental changes in the scheme of the levy of wealth tax in India from the Assessment Year 1993-94. Wealth tax is leviable on the net wealth tax of individuals, HUFs and companies only. All items of wealth tax are not liable to wealth tax now. Under the provisions of Section 3 wealth tax is chargeable at the flat rate of 1% of the amount by which the net wealth tax exceeds Rs. 15 lakhs with effect from Assessment Year 1993-94. The expression "net wealth" refers to assets only. The expression "assets" according to a new clause (ea) of Section 2 (2) of the Wealth Tax Act as amended by the Finance (No. 2) Act, 1998, with effect from the A.Y. 1999-2000 meant, broadly speaking, the following types of non-productive assets on which wealth tax is leviable:

1. Any guest house and any residential building or land appurtenant thereto (other than any residential property let out for a minimum of 300 days), a farm house situated within 25 kms from the local limits of any municipality. However, it does not include a house meant exclusively for residential purposes and which is allotted by a company to an employee or an officer or a Director who is in whole time employment, with a gross annual salary of less than Rs. 5 lakh. Likewise, any house for residential or commercial purposes which forms part of the stock-in-trade is also not considered liable to wealth tax. Similarly, any house which the assessee may occupy for the purpose of any business or profession carried on by him is also exempt from wealth tax.

2. Motor cars (other than those used by the assessee in the business and running them on hire or as stock-in-trade)

3. Jewellery, furniture, utensils or any other article made fully or partially of gold, silver, platinum or any other precious metal or any alloy containing one or more of these precious metals.

Where, however, any of these items is used by the assessee as a stock-in-trade, it is not liable to wealth tax.

4. Yachts, boats, aircrafts (other than those used by the assessee for commercial purposes)

5. Urban land

6. Cash in hand in excess of Rs. 50,000 for individuals and HUFs and in the case of other persons any amount not recorded in the books of account.

Thus it is clear that other assets which are not covered under the above category are not liable to wealth tax in India. Thus some of the important items of wealth which were earlier either fully taxable or partially taxable to wealth tax are now completely exempt from the purview of wealth tax with effect from Assessment Year 1993-94:

(a) Bank fixed deposits
(b) Units of the UTI
(c) Units of Mutual Funds
(d) Government securities
(e) Loans and advances
(f) Shares and debentures
(g) Industrial assets, etc.

The expression "Urban land" means any land situated in any area comprised within the jurisdiction of the Municipality or a Cantonment Board which has a population of not less then 10,000, as per the latest published figures or any land situated in any area within 8 km, from the local limits of any Municipality or Cantonment Board as is notified by the Central Government. However, urban land does not include land on which construction of a building is not permissible under any law for the time being in the area in which such land is situated or land occupied by any building which has been constructed with the approval of the appropriate authority or any unused land held by the assessee for industrial purposes for a period of two years from the date of its acquisition by him or any land held by the assessee as stock-in-trade for a period of 10 years from the date of its acquisition.

3. Specific exemptions

Section 5 of the Wealth Tax Act contains a list of certain specific exemptions. The long list of various exemptions, with effect from the Assessment Year 1993-94, has been curtailed. Thus from a practical point of view certain important general types of complete exemptions from wealth tax under Section 5 of the Wealth Tax Act are the following:

1. Any property held by the taxpayer under trust or any other legal obligation for any public purposes of charitable or religious nature in India.
2. The interest of the assessee in the co-parcenary property of any HUF of which he is a member. Co-parcenary means joint heirship.
3. Any one building in the occupation of a Ruler.
4. One house or part of a house or a plot of land not exceeding 500 sq. metres in area belonging to the assessee from the A.Y. 1999-2000.
5. Jewellery in the possession of a former Ruler.
6. In the case of an NRI who is ordinarily residing in a foreign country, who, on leaving that country, has returned to India with the intention of permanently residing therein, money or the value of assets brought by him to India and the value of assets acquired by him out of such money within one year immediately preceding the date of his return or at any time thereafter.

However, this exemption would apply only for a period of seven successive assessment years commencing on the Assessment Year next following the date on which such a person returns to India. As regards NRI Account Deposits and FCNR Deposits, as also shares, etc., held by the NRI they are not considered as "Assets" and are thus absolutely exempt from wealth tax. Thus an NRI is not liable to any wealth tax at all on shares, units, bank deposits, government securities, gold bond deposits, loans and advances, etc. held by him.

4. Clubbing of the wealth with the income of the parents

Under the provisions of Section 64 (1A) of the Income Tax Act, as described elsewhere in this book, the wealth tax of a minor child (other than a disabled child) is also to clubbed under Section 4 of the Wealth Tax Act with the wealth of that parent whose wealth is higher. Where, however, the marriage of the parents of the minor child does not subsist, the clubbing of the net wealth tax of the child has to be done with the net wealth tax of the parent who maintains the minor child in the relevant previous year.

5. Assets and tax outside India are not to be calculated while computing taxable wealth tax

It is provided in Section 6 that in computing the net wealth tax of an individual who is not a citizen of India or a Hindu Undivided Family not resident in India or resident but not ordinarily resident in India, during the year ending on the valuation date, the following items are not to be taken into account:

> The value of the assets and debts located outside India and the value of the assets in India represented by any loans or debts owing to the assessee, in any case where the interest, if any, payable on such loans or debts is not to be included in the total income of the assessee under Section 10 of the Income Tax Act (as described in Chapter 4 in detail). Generally speaking, a non-resident would be liable to wealth tax on non-productive Indian assets only. Here also those assets which are located in India but which are represented by loans or assets in respect of which interest is totally exempt, are not to be considered taxable assets for the purposes of wealth tax.

Special procedure of assessment regarding income of an NRI from foreign exchange assets

1. Introduction

A study of the preceding paras shows that a non-resident Indian enjoys several income tax exemptions while computing his taxable income under the Income Tax Act. There are certain additional deductions which are allowed while computing the total income. These are in respect of certain items which deserve special treatment and which are deductible from the gross total income as explained in Chapter 8. It is only after giving effect to the exemptions as well as the various deductions that the total income is computed. If such total income exceeds Rs. 1,00,000 for the A.Y. 2007-08 or Rs. 1,10,000 for the A. Y. 2008-2009, then only does a non-resident Indian become liable to pay income tax in India like any other resident individual. Thus on the total income (i.e., after excluding the various exemptions and deductions allowable under the different provisions of the Income Tax Act) of Rs. 2,50,000 for the Assessment Year 2007-2008 the total income tax payable by a non-resident Indian is only Rs. 25,000. For the A.Y. 2008-2009, such tax would be Rs. 24,000 only. This would be increased by two cesses for education, namely 2% of the income tax as education cess and 1% of the income tax as secondary & higher educaion cess. It is like the income tax payable by a resident individual. There are, however, certain types of investment income of a non-resident Indian where there is a special procedure of assessment under which a non-resident Indian is not liable to income tax in India at the slab rates of income tax but is liable to income tax at a special ad-hoc rate which is 20% (& 10% on long-term capital gains) on the entire total income without any deduction of any type under any provision of the Act. Thus, there is no risk of the non-resident Indian becoming liable to the maximum rate of income tax of 30% which is applicable to a taxpayer on a total income in excess of Rs. 2,50,000. If a non-resident opts for the special procedure he would be liable to income tax only at 20% whatever may be the quantum of such total income. This and several other aspects related to the computation of total income and the tax payable by the non-resident on the special investment income are discussed in this chapter. These are based on Chapter XII-A of the Income Tax Act, which contains Sections 115C to 115-I. Reference to the sections in the chapter are of this Act only.

2. Special provision of computation of the total income of a non-resident Indian

It is provided in Section 115D that no deduction in respect of any expenditure or allowance shall be allowed under any provision of the Income Tax Act in computing the investment income of a non-resident Indian. It is further provided that in the case of a non-resident Indian, where his gross total income consists only of investment income or income by way of long-term capital gains or both, no deduction would be allowed under Chapter VI-A of the Income Tax Act (which are explained in detail in Chapter 8 of this book). Further nothing contained in the second proviso to Section 48 would apply to capital gains of NRIs. It is also mentioned in the Income Tax Act that where the gross total income of a non-resident Indian includes any income of the type mentioned above, the total income shall be reduced by the amount of such income and if any deductions under Chapter VI-A of the Income Tax Act are to be allowed then they would be allowed as if the gross total income as so reduced were the gross total income of the assessee. Thus, this special provision is applicable where a non-resident Indian has certain investment income or has investment income as well as other income.

3. Who is a non-resident Indian for the purposes of these special provisions ?

The special provisions relating to certain incomes of non-resident Indians according to Chapter XII-A of the Income Tax Act are applicable only to non-resident Indians. These provisions are aimed to give special tax concessions on certain investments in respect of income tax which is levied at a special rate on the income of those investments of non-resident Indians. Hence, it is very important to know the meaning of the expression "non-resident Indian". According to Section 115C(e) a "non-resident Indian" means an individual, being a citizen of India, or a person of Indian origin who is not a resident. A person is deemed to be of Indian origin if he or either of his parents or any of his grand-parents were born in undivided India. In Chapter 1, topic 5 we have defined and explained a "resident person". In topic 3 of Chapter 1 we have explained the meaning of "non-resident". Reference may be made to those paras for understanding the meaning of the expression "resident" and "non-resident". It may also be mentioned here that Article 8 of the Constitution of India provides that any person who, or either whose parents, or any of whose grand-parents was born in India, who is ordinarily resident in any country outside India, would be deemed to be a citizen of India if he is registered by the diplomatic or consular representative of India in the country where he is for the time being resident. For this purpose an application has to made in the prescribed form and manner. Thus, generally speaking a non-resident Indian would mean a citizen of India who is not resident in India as well as persons who are of Indian origin, who are not resident in India. This expression is broadly understood by almost all the non-resident Indians clearly. It is such non-resident Indians who enjoy special tax concessions relating to the computation of income tax of certain investment incomes, etc., which is explained in this chapter.

4. Specified foreign exchange assets income from which is eligible for the special provisions of assessment

It is not that every type of income of a non-resident Indian is entitled to the uniform rate of income tax of 20%. It is only certain selected assets, the income of which alone would be liable to the special provisions of assessment in the case of non-resident Indians. Such assets are known as "foreign exchange asset". Under Section 115C(b) "foreign exchange assets" would mean any specified asset which the assessee has acquired or purchased or subscribed with or subscribed in a convertible foreign exchange. The expression "convertible foreign exchange", according to Section 115C(a) means, foreign exchange which is for the time being treated by the Reserve Bank of India as convertible foreign exchange for the purposes of Foreign Exchange Regulation Act 1973, and any rules made under it. Investment income means any income which is derived from foreign exchange assets. As stated earlier, the sections referred to in this para and other paras of the chapter are of the Income

Tax Act 1961, unless otherwise so specified. Under Section 115C(f) "specified assets" means any of the following assets, namely,

(i) Shares in an Indian company;
(ii) debentures issued by an Indian company, which is not a private company as defined in the Companies Act 1956;
(iii) deposits with an Indian company which is not a private company as defined in the Companies Act 1956;
(iv) any security of the Central Government as defined in Section 2(2) of the Public Debts Act 1944;
(v) such other assets as the Central Government may specify in this behalf by notification in the official gazette.

Thus, only five types of assets acquired or purchased out of convertible foreign exchange can be termed as specified assets, more popularly known as "foreign exchange assets". It is the investment income from such foreign exchange assets which alone is entitled to a special treatment under Chapter XII-A of the Income Tax Act as explained in this para and other paras of this chapter.

5. Income tax on investment income and long-term capital gains of an NRI

Section 115E provides for the levy of income tax on the investment income and long-term capital gains of a non-resident Indian. It is provided that if the total income of a non-resident Indian consists only of investment income or income by way of long-term capital gains relating to long-term foreign exchange assets, then income tax would be payable on the long-term capital gains @ 10% and @ 20% on investment income.

Thus, as per Section 115E income tax @ 10% only would be charged in respect of long-term capital gains arising any of the assets mentioned in "specified assets" as per para 4 above. However, the long-term capital gains on non-specified assets, like property, land, jewellery, etc. would be charged @ 20%.

6. When is no income tax payable on the long-term capital gains of foreign exchange assets?

Section 115F provides for complete exemption of long-term capital gains on the transfer of foreign exchange assets in certain cases. Thus, it is provided that where, in the case of a non-resident Indian, any long-term capital gains arise from the transfer of a foreign exchange asset and the non-resident Indian has within a period of six months from the date of such transfer invested or deposited the whole or any part of the net consideration in any specified asset, namely the assets as mentioned in para 4 above, or in account referred to in Section 10(4) or in Savings Certificates as per Section 10(4B) (explained in detail in Chapter 4, topics 2 and 3), then no tax is payable. Thus, if the amount of the net consideration is invested in the purchase of a new asset as specified earlier, then no income tax is leviable on such long-term capital gains. Where, however, the cost of the new asset is less than the net consideration in respect of the original asset, then income tax is to be levied on the proportionate capital gain.

The expression "net consideration" in relation to the transfer of the original asset means the full value of the consideration received or accruing as a result of the transfer of such assets as reduced by any expenditure incurred wholly and exclusively in connection with such transfer. It is also provided in sub-Section (2) of Section 115F where the net asset is transferred or converted into money within a period of three years from the date of its acquisition, the amount of capital gains arising from the transfer of the original assets not so charged under Section 45 on the basis of the cost of such new asset as provided in this Section, it would be deemed to be income chargeable under the head "capital gains" relating to the long-term capital asset of the previous year in which the new asset is transferred or converted into money. Thus, long-term capital gains can be completely income tax free if they are invested in specified assets or other assets as mentioned above. A non-resident Indian should take full advantage of this provision by adopting proper tax planning.

7. A non-resident Indian need not file any income tax return in certain cases

A very important privilege is granted to a non-resident Indian who has income from foreign exchange assets only. Thus, it is provided in Section 115G that a non-resident Indian is not required by Section 139(1) to file an income tax return, if both the conditions as given below are fulfilled, namely:

(a) his total income in respect of which he is assessable under the Income Tax Act during the previous year consisted only of investment income or income by way of long-term capital gains or both; and

(b) the tax deductible at source under the provisions of Chapter XVII has been deducted from such income.

Thus, it is clear that where the requisite income tax is deducted at source from the income of a non-resident Indian and he has only investment income or long-term capital gains relating to foreign exchange assets, he is not required to furnish any income tax return.

8. When does the special procedure continue to apply to a person even after he becomes a resident in India?

Sometimes a non-resident Indian may become resident in India in any subsequent year. Normally a resident is not entitled to the special tax concession under Chapter XII-A of the Income Tax Act relating to the assessment of the total income being investment income of foreign exchange assets at the 20% rate of income tax. But under the provisions of Section 115H, such a non-resident Indian who becomes a resident in respect of the total income of any subsequent year can also continue to be assessable to income tax at the special rate of 20% income tax on the investment income in future years as well. For this purpose he has to exercise his option. Where such a non-resident Indian becomes a resident in India in a subsequent year and wishes to avail himself of the special provisions of Chapter XII-A, he should furnish to the Assessing Officer a declaration in writing along with his return of income under Section 139 for the assessment year for which he is assessable to the effect that the provisions of Chapter XII-A would continue to apply to him in respect of the investment income from any foreign exchange asset. However, only the last four items of the specified assets as mentioned in topic 4 above, would enjoy this special concession. Thus, in respect of the income from investment in shares of a limited company a non-resident Indian will not get the privilege of this tax concession under Chapter XII-A when he becomes a resident. He would, however, be eligible to the tax concession in respect of the income from the investments from the assets of the four types mentioned in Section 115C(f)(ii) or (iii) or (iv) or (v).

9. NRIs have the option not to be governed by the special provisions

The provisions of Chapter XII-A, namely, levy of a uniform rate of income tax of 20% on the investment income of a non-resident Indian, etc. are not compulsory in the case of every non-resident Indian. Rather, Section 115-I provides that a non-resident Indian may elect not to be governed by the provisions in this chapter in any financial year. He may do so when he finds that the normal rates of income tax would mean a lower income tax liability than the uniform rate of 20%. Such a case would exist there when the total income is a little over Rs. 2,00,000. The average rate of income tax on such an income would be about 20%. Hence a non-resident Indian with an income of less than Rs. 2,00,000 would certainly like to be assessed by the normal procedure and according to the normal rates of income tax. In such a case he has to furnish to the Assessing Officer a return of income for the relevant year declaring that the provisions of Chapter XII-A would not be applicable to him for that assessment year. When the non-resident does such a thing for any assessment year the provisions of Chapter XII-A would not apply to him for that assessment year and his total income for that assessment year would be computed and tax on such total income would be charged in accordance with the other provisions of the Income Tax Act.

10. Tax planning guidelines for an NRI having income from foreign exchange assets as well as other income

When a non-resident Indian has income from foreign exchange assets as well as other income, tax planning assumes special significance. A calculation has to be made by the non-resident of the income tax payable on the investment income out of such foreign exchange assets. In the case of a large investment it would generally be prudent for him to be liable to income tax according to the special provisions of Chapter XII-A @ 20% income tax only. As regards his other income, he would be liable to income tax on the usual slab rates of tax. Where, however, the non-resident finds that the investment income is below Rs. 2,00,000 it would be better for him to be taxed like a resident individual. If this tax planning is adopted by him he would pay less tax.

CHAPTER 8

Deductions and rebates allowed to NRIs in computation of total income and tax payable

1. Introduction

In Chapter 7 we saw that a non-resident Indian is not allowed any deduction under Chapter VI-A of the Income Tax Act in the computation of his taxable total income which is by way of investment income from foreign exchange assets. This is a general rule and is applicable to the entire investment income of all non-resident Indians. However, a non-resident Indian, as explained in topic 9 of the preceding chapter can opt not to be governed by the special provisions relating to taxation of the investment income at the uniform rate of 20%, but be governed by the general provisions of the Income Tax Act, whereby income tax is levied on the Indian income of a non-resident Indian at the slab rates of income tax. Further, even in the case of a non-resident Indian, tax at the uniform rate of 20% on income from house property etc., to which the special provisions of Chapter XII-A of the Income Tax Act do not apply, is not leviable. In the case of such income, it is not the gross income which is liable to income tax, but the net income, after deducting the expenses for earning such income as also certain other deductions, as explained in Chapter VI-A of the Income Tax Act. The resultant net total income alone is liable to income tax. It is, therefore, very important for a non-resident Indian to be familiar with the important deductions that are allowed in the computation of total income as per the special provisions of Chapter VI-A of the Income Tax Act. In this Chapter, we deal with the most significant of such deductions and rebates which are relevant not merely for the non-resident Indian alone but for the resident Indian as well to the extent that they are equally applicable for the non-resident Indians. Only those deductions which have a real and significant bearing to the computation of the total income have been described in this Chapter. Sections referred to in this chapter are of the Income Tax Act.

2. Gross total income

It is the gross total income from which the various deductions as given in Chapter VI-A of the Income Tax Act are allowed. Hence it is very important for a non-resident to know the meaning of the expression "gross total income". Section 80B(5) defines "gross total income" as the total income computed in accordance with the provisions of the Income Tax Act, before making any deduction under Chapter VI-A. Thus, for finding out the gross total income we have to compute the total income of the non-resident Indian first. In computing the total income under each head of income, the expenditure allowed in computing the taxable income under the relevant head is to be deducted. For example, while computing income from house property one-fifth of the annual value as deduction for repairs and collection charges, whether incurred or not, is to be allowed deduction to arrive at the net taxable income from house property. The total of all the heads of income before making any deduction under Chapter VI-A would be the gross total income.

Illustration No. 28

B has the following income in respect of the previous year relevant to the Assessment Year 2008-2009:

		Rs.
(1)	Net income from house property situated at Delhi	90,000
(2)	Interest on Relief Bonds	30,000
(3)	Short-term capital gains	27,000

The gross total income of B for the Assessment Year 2007-2008 will be computed as follows:

(1)	Income from house property	90,000
(2)	Interest on Relief Bonds (fully exempt)	—
(3)	Short-term capital gains	27,000
	Gross total income	1,17,000

Thus, for the Assessment Year 2008-2009, no income tax would be paid on the first Rs 1,10,000 out of Rs 1,17,000. The balance of income of Rs. 7,000 would be taxable at 10%, i.e. Rs. 700 total tax. This would be increased by 20% Ed. Cess and 1% Secondary and Higher Ed. Cess on I.T., i.e., Rs 21.

---

3. Tax benefit regarding life insurance premium, PPF contributions, NSCs, tuition fees, etc.

A deduction as per Section 80C from income upto Rs. 1,00,000 for payments made by an Individual or Hindu Undivided Family in respect of any one or more of the following [without any sub-limit for any Investment] is allowed:

1. Payment for Life Insurance Premium.
2. Payment for Deferred Annuity Plan.
3. Deferred Annuity payable by Government.
4. Contribution to Public Provident Fund.
5. Contribution to Provident Fund set up by Central Government.
6. Contribution to Recognized Provident Fund.
7. Contribution to Recognized Superannuation Fund.
8. Subscription to any security or deposit notified by Government.
9. Subscription to Savings Certificates.
10. Subscription for Unit-Linked Insurance Plan, 1971.
11. Contribution for Unit Linked Insurance Plan of LIC Mutual Fund.
12. Payment for Annuity Plan of LIC or any other insurer.
13. Subscription to units of Notified Mutual Funds.
14. Contribution to Notified Pension Fund of Mutual Fund.
15. Pension fund set up by National Housing Bank.
16. Subscription to Deposit Scheme of Public Sector Company engaged in providing long-term finance for house.
17. Tuition fees of two children in India.
18. Payment of instalment for self-financing for a residential property or repayment of loan.
19. Subscription to equity shares or debentures as approved (for infrastructure).
20. Subscription to any units of Mutual Fund as approved by the Central Board of Direct Taxes.
21. Five-year Bank Fixed Deposit with conditions (from A.Y. 2007-08).
22. Notified Bonds issued by NABARD

Note: 1. Total amount allowed as deduction is limited to Rs. 1 lakh inclusive of deduction as per Section 80C, 80CCC, 80 CCD and 80CCE.
2. The investment for the above purpose can be made out of any funds available with the assessee and not necessarily out of the income chargeable to tax.
3. This deduction is available irrespective of the income of the year.

4. From the A.Y. 2007-08 contributions to Pension Plan under Section 80CCC would be permissible as a deduction upto Rs. 1 lakh but within the overall limit of deduction under Section 80C.

4. Deduction for donations to certain funds and charitable institutions

Under the provisions of Section 80G, a non-resident Indian, like any other taxpayer, is entitled to a deduction of the qualifying amount of donation in computing his total income. The important Funds which qualify for such deduction are Jawaharlal Nehru Memorial Fund or the Prime Minister's Relief Fund or the Prime Minister's National Relief Fund or the Indira Gandhi Memorial Trust, etc or any other Fund or any institution exempt under Section 80G. Contribution to the Prime Minister's National Relief Fund, the P.M. Armenia Earthquake Relief Fund, the Africa (Public Contributions — India), a University or any approved educational institution of national eminence, the Zila Saksharta Samiti, the National Blood Transfusion Council, etc., N.F. for Communal Harmony, National Illness Assistance Fund, C.M./L.G. Relief Fund, National Sports Fund (from A.Y. 1999-2000) contribution to the Government, certain approved institutions, etc., for family planning and the Fund for Technology Development and Application set up by the Central Government (from the A.Y. 2000-2001), donations for Kargil jawans (from the A.Y. 2000-2001) and the National Trust for Welfare of persons with Autism, Cerebral Palsy Mental Retardation and Multiple Disabilities (from the A.Y. 2002-2003) is entitled to deduction @ 100% of the donation. In all other cases the rate of deduction is 50% of the donation. As regards the maximum eligible deduction there is no limit regarding donation to the National Defence Fund or Jawaharlal Nehru Memorial Fund or the Prime Minister's National Relief Fund or the Prime Minister's Drought Relief Fund or the Prime Minister's Armenia Earthquake Relief Fund or the Africa (Public Contributions-India) Fund or the National Children's Fund or the Indira Gandhi Memorial Trust or the Rajiv Gandhi Foundation or the National Foundation for Communal Harmony or National Illness Assistance Fund or a University or an approved educational institution or any Zila Saksharta Samiti or the National Blood Transfusion Council or any State Blood Transfusion Council or any fund set up by a State Govt. to provide medical relief to the poor or to Army, Naval or Air Force Welfare Funds. In respect of all other donations like donation to a charitable institution exempt under Section 80G, the maximum amount of donation eligible for deduction is 10% of the gross total income (as reduced by any other sum on which income tax is not payable under the Income Tax Act and any sum in respect of which the assessee is entitled to deduction under Chapter VI-A, as discussed in this Chapter), whichever is less. No deduction is allowed on donation in kind.

5. Deduction in respect of interest on securities, bank interest, etc. upto the A.Y. 2005-06 only

A non-resident Indian, like any other resident individual, was entitled to a deduction under Section 80L up to a maximum of Rs. 15,000 for the Assessment Year 2004-2005 and A.Y. 2005-2006. This included Rs. 3,000 reserved exclusively for interest on government securities.

As per the Finance Act, 2005, this deduction is not permissible on and from the A.Y. 2006-07.

6. Deduction in respect of profits and gains from a new industrial undertaking or infrastructural facility

Under the provisions of Section 80-IB a partial tax holiday is allowed in respect of the profits and gains of a new industrial undertaking set up on or after 1.4.1991 and before 1.4.1995, or an approved hotel which starts functioning from that date. In the case of companies, 30% of the profits derived from new industrial undertakings, etc., is deductible from the gross total income for a period of ten years; in the case of other assessees (including non-residents) 25% of such profits will be deductible for a like period. The benefit of "tax holiday" is admissible to all small-scale industrial undertakings irrespective of the type of their manufacturing activity. An industrial undertaking is regarded as a small-scale industrial undertaking if the aggregate value of the plant and machinery installed, on the last day of the previous year, for the purpose of the business of the undertaking does not exceed Rs. 60 lakhs. In the case of other industrial undertakings it is allowed only if the new industrial undertaking is not engaged in the production of articles listed in the 11th schedule to the Income Tax Act. There are certain other requirements for the eligibility for this deduction.

A 10-year tax holiday for any enterprise which builds, maintains or operates any infrastructure facility such as roads, highways, express ways, water treatment system, solid waste management, new bridges, airports, inland waterways and inland ports and rapid rail transport systems on BOT or BOOT or similar other basis on or after 1.4.1995 would be allowed under Section 80IA. Likewise, SSI industrial units, commencing production on or after 1.4.95 and any time before 31.3.2002 would also be allowed partial tax holiday of 25% or 30% for 10 years out of an initial period of 15 years.

A five-year tax holiday under Section 80-IB of the Income Tax Act, 1961, to approved companies engaged in scientific and industrial research and development activities on commercial lines is allowed. This incentive shall be available to any company that has as its main objective, activities in the areas of scientific and industrial research and development and which has been accorded approval by the prescribed authority, namely, Secretary, Department of Scientific and Industrial Research. This tax holiday shall be available to any company, whether new or existing, which is accorded approval by the aforesaid prescribed authority at any time before 1.4.2007. The 100% deduction for a five-year period, shall commence from the assessment year relevant to the previous year in which the approval by the prescribed authority is accorded to such a company.

The benefit of tax holiday under Section 80-IA, to other infrastructure facilities like water supply projects, irrigation systems, sanitation and sewerage systems has also been extended. Please see paras 7, 8 and 9.

The Finance Act, 2002 had, with effect from the A.Y. 2003-2004, provided the grant of deduction under Section 80-IA(2) to an undertaking which develops and operates or maintains and operates a Special Economic Zone. Besides, separate audit for undertakings claiming deduction under Sections 80-IA and 80-IB has also been made mandatory for companies and co-operative societies. Also see para 11 of Chapter 4.

The deduction allowed at 100% of the profits for ten assessment years of a scientific research and development company would be so allowed even where the approval by the prescribed authority is received before 31.3.2012.

7. Tax holiday to enterprises providing telecommunication services, industrial parks, new hotels and having commercial production of mineral oil

A new provision has been made to provide for 100% deduction from the profits and gains of an assessee engaged in the business of providing tele-communication services for the initial five assessment years. A deduction of 25% (30% in the case of companies) from such profits and gains will be allowed for a further period of five years. Thus, the total period of tax holiday will be 10 years. This deduction will be allowed to an undertaking which begins to provide the telecommunication services at any time during the period beginning on 1.4.1995 and ending on 31st March, 2005.

Another amendment relates to the extension of the tax holiday to industrial parks notified for this purpose, in accordance with any scheme framed by the Central Government. Vide Notification No. S.O. 193(E) dated 30.3.1999 an Industrial Park/Industrial Model Town Scheme has been notified. This tax holiday will encourage investments in industrial infrastructure. Those industrial parks which start operating during the period beginning on 1st April, 1997 and ending on 31.3.2009 will be eligible for 100% deduction for 10 assessment years.

Another amendment relates to the deduction equal to 50% of the profits of hotels which are located in a hilly or rural area or a place of pilgrimage or where tourism infrastructure needs to be developed. This will be allowed for a period of ten assessment years to hotels which start functioning at any time during the period from 1.4.1997 to 31.3.2001. In respect of hotels located at any other place, the deduction shall be 30% of the profits. However, the hotels located in the metropolitan cities of Calcutta, Chennai (Madras), Delhi and Mumbai (Bombay) will not be eligible for this tax deduction. This amendment will be effective from the A.Y. 1998-99 and subsequent years. Such hotels must be owned by a limited company only, having a paid up capital of not less than Rs. 5 lakh. Profits of agro-based industries would also be exempt u/s 80IB (11A).

From the A.Y. 1998-99 an undertaking having commercial production of mineral oil in the North-Eastern States of India would be eligible to 100% tax holiday for a period of initial seven assessment years.

The Finance Act, 1999 had extended the benefit of tax holiday for undertakings setting up new transmission lines on or after 1.4.1999 but before 1.4.2003 to profits derived therefrom as are available from power generation undertakings. Industries in notified areas in North-East States would enjoy full tax holiday for ten assessment years, under new Section 10C inserted by the Finance Act, 1999 from the A.Y. 1999-2000 and under Section 80IC inserted by the Finance Act, 2003 from the A.Y. 2004-2005.

8. Five year tax holiday for new industrial undertakings in industrially backward areas & districts

The Finance Act 1993 with effect from the Assessment Year 1994-95, had provided that any new industrial undertaking located in an industrially backward State or Union Territory as specified in the 8th schedule or set up in any part of India for the generation and distribution of power will be completely exempt from income tax to the extent of 100% of the profits and gains derived from such industrial undertaking for the initial five assessment years. Of course such new industrial undertaking or power plant should begin manufacturing or producing articles on or after 1.4.1993 and before 1.4.2000, later on increased to 31.3.2002. Thus, a power plant can be set up in any part of India so as to become eligible for a 5-year tax holiday. But a new industrial undertaking to be eligible for a complete tax holiday for the first five years must be located in an industrially backward area as specified in the 8th schedule which broadly relate to Arunachal, Assam, Goa, Manipur, Meghalaya. Mizoram, Nagaland, Sikkim, Tripura, Union Territory of Andaman & Nicobar Islands, J&K, Pondicherry, Lakshadeep, D. & N. Haveli, etc.

A good deal of tax saving can be achieved through proper tax planning by starting a new industrial undertaking in the industrially backward areas or a new power plant in any part of India.

From the Assessment Year 1995-96 similar tax holiday would be available on a new industrial undertaking in any notified very Backward District manufacturing, etc. between 1.10.1994 to 31.3.2002. Vide Notification No. S.O. 440(E) dated 15.6.1999, 52 Category "A" and 70 Category "B" Districts have been notified [see (1999) 238 ITR 14 st.]. Likewise, the Income Tax (Amendment) Act, 1998 also made more changes.

The Finance Act 2002 had further extended the period from 31.3.2002 to 31.3.2004 by which if any new industrial undertaking is set up in a backward State or backward District, then it will be eligible to the tax holiday as it allowed to other industries set up earlier, namely 100% tax holiday for five years and 25% or 30% for the balance five years.

9. New incentives for infrastructure development and industrialisation — Section 80-IA

The Finance (No. 2) Act, 1998 made a number of amendments in the scheme of tax-holiday under Section 80-IA.

The Finance Act, 1999 substituted Section 80IA by two Sections 80IA and 80IB. The newly substituted Section 80IB(10) provides this tax holiday would be available for housing projects in areas other than falling in and within 25 kms. from the municipal limits of Delhi and Mumbai where the built-up area of dwelling units may be upto a maximum limit of 1,500 sq. ft. instead of 1,000 sq.ft. if the same is approved by 31.3.2005. These are tabulated below for easy reference (Tables 1 and 2).

Table 1
Tax Holiday

Extent of deduction & other conditions regarding new industrial under-takings, hotels, etc. u/s 80-IB (up-to-date)

Sl. No.	Type of Business	Rate of deduction	Period of deduction	Period of setting up business, etc.
1.	Industrial undertaking (Non-SSI & cold storage plant)	30% for companies & 25% for others	10 years 12 years (For co-operatives)	1.4.1991 to 31.3.1995
2.	SSI undertaking or other cold storage plant	-do-	-do-	1.4.1995 to 31.3.2002
3.	Industrial undertaking in Backward States (8th Schedule) [No deduction to industrial undertaking in J & K manufacturing Articles specified in the Thirteenth Schedule	100% 30% for companies (25% for others)	Initial 5 years next 5 years (next 7 years for co-operatives)	1.4.1993 to 31.3.2004 31.3.2012 (J.&K.)
4.	Notified industries in N.E. Region	100%	10 years	—
5.	Category "A" Ind. Backward Districts	100% 30% for companies & 25% for others	5 years Next 5 years (next 7 years for co-operatives)	1.10.1994 to 31.3.2004
6.	Category "B" Ind. Backward Districts	100% 30% for companies & 25% for others	3 years Next 5 years (next 9 years for co-operatives)	1.10.1994 to 31.3.2004
7.	Ship	30%	10 years	1.4.1991 to 31.3.1995

Contd...

Sl. No.	Type of Business	Rate of deduction	Period of deduction	Period of setting up business, etc.
8.	Hotel in a hilly area, rural area, etc.	50%	10 years	1.4.1990 to 31.3.1995 & 1.4.1997 to 31.3.2001
9.	Hotel in any other place (other than Kolkatta, Chennai, Delhi or Mumbai)	30%	10 years	1.4.1991 to 31.3.1995 & 1.4.1997 to 31.3.2001
10.	Multiplex Theatre	50%	5 years	1.4.2002 to 31.3.2005
11.	Companies carrying on scientific research and development	100%	10 years	Approval before 1.4.2007
12.	Mineral oil production	100%	7 years	From 1.4.1997
13.	Mineral oil refining	100%	7 years	From 1.10.1998
14.	Special Housing Projects on 1 acre land	100%	Relevant years [Approval before 31.3.2007]	From 1.10.1998
15.	Cold chain facility for agricultural produce	a) 100% b) 30% for companies & 25% for others	Initial 5 years Next 5 years (7 years for co-operatives)	1.4.1999 to 31.3.2004
16.	Integrated business of handling, storage and transportation of food grains or processing presentation & packaging of fruits and vegetables	a) -do- b) -do- 100%	Initial 5 years Next 5 years Initial 5 years	From 1.4.2001 From 1.4.2004
17.	Rural Hospital with atleast 100 beds			From 1.10.2004 to 31.3.2008

Table 2

Deduction for Infrastructure Facilities, etc. u/s 80-IA

The eligibility of deduction u/s 80-IA 100% deduction for 10 years. The 10 Year consecutive period at the option of assessee is out of initial 15 years for a port, airport, inland waterway or inland port and 20 years for highway project or roads, etc.). For 3 and 4 it is 5 year tax holiday and 30% for the next 5 years.

Sl. No.	Type of Infrastructure Enterprise	Period of Development Operation etc.
1.	Any assessee developing, operating and maintaining an infrastructure facility	From 1.4.1995

Contd.. .

Sl. No.	Type of Infrastructure Enterprise	Period of Development Operation etc.
2.	Any assessee developing or operating or developing, operating and maintaining an infrastructure facility	From 1.4.2001
3.	Any undertaking providing telecommunication services including broad and internet service	1.4.1995 to 31.3.2005
4.	Any undertaking for developing special Economic Zones	1.4.2001 to 31.3.2006
5.	Any undertaking developing and operating an industrial park	1.4.1997 to 31.3.2009
6.	Any undertaking operating and maintaining an industrial park [Extended by the Finance Act, 2006]	1.4.1999 to 31.3.2009
7.	Any undertaking for generation and/or distribution of power [Extended by the Finance Act, 2006]	1.4.1993 to 31.3.2010
8.	A- Any undertaking starting transmission or distribution lines	1.4.1999 to 31.3.2010
	B-Renovation and modernation of transmission or distribution lines or operation of a cross-country natural gas distribution network from 1.4.07 (added by Finance Act, 2007)	1.4.2004 to 31.3.2010

Meaning of Infrastructure Facility
[as per Expln. to Section 80-1A(4)]
It means—
(a) A road including toll road, a bridge or a rail system;
(b) A highway project including housing or other activities being its integral part;
(c) A water supply project, water treatment system, irrigation project, sanitation and sewerage system or solid waste management system;
(d) A port, airport, inland waterway or inland port or navigational channel in the sea.

10. Liberalisation of tax holiday provision for infrastructure, telecom services, power generation, special economic zones, industrial parks, etc.— Section 80-IA

Various modifications were made to Section 80-IA by the Finance Act, 2001 from the A.Y. 2002-2003 and by the Finance Act, 2006 to provide incentives for infrastructure, etc. These modifications in brief are:

(a) The existing two-tier benefit to provide a 10-year tax holiday is replaced by a new provision that for an infrastructure facility in the nature of a road, including a toll road, bridge, rail system, highway project, water supply project, sanitation, sewerage and solid waste management system, a 10-year tax holiday may be availed consecutively out of 20 years beginning from the year in which the undertaking begins operating the infrastructure facility.

(b) An identical 10-year tax holiday may be availed in a block of 15 years in the case of other infrastructure, namely, for airport, port, inland port and inland waterways.

(c) The mandatory requirements that such infrastructure facility shall be transferred to the Central Government, State Government, local authority or any other statutory authority, has been removed.

(d) The two-tier benefit available to undertakings in telecommunication services is reintroduced and it is extended to internet service providers and broadband networks, for those undertakings which provide the services on or before 31.3.2004.

(e) The tax holiday period to undertakings commencing generation of power or laying a network of new transmission and distribution lines on or before 31.3.2010 would be allowed for a 10-year period in place of the two-tier benefit out of the initial 15 years.

(f) The tax benefit available to the developers of industrial parks has been extended to the developers of Special Economic Zones.

Thus, this benefit would be available to the developers of new special economic zones and also to developers of industrial parks if such industrial parks are developed on or before 31.3.2009. Further, the tax holiday period would be ten-year period which could be availed in ten consecutive assessment years in a block of fifteen years.

The ten-year tax holiday benefit is extended to include a navigational channel in the sea as laying and operating, cross-country gas distribution network, including gas pipeline and storage facilities being an integral part of the network. This amendment is made by the Finance Act. 2007, effective from the A.Y. 2008-2009. Amalgamation or merger on or after 1.4.2007 would not entitle the benefit of Section 801A.

Tax benefit u/s 10AA would be given only to promote new industry and new investment in SEZs and not to facilitate migration of existing industries by splitting up or the reconstitution of an already existing business, etc. This amendment is made by the Finance Act, 2007 with retrospective effect from 10.2.2006.

11. Ten year tax holiday in respect of certain undertakings in Himachal Pradesh, Sikkim, Uttaranchal and N.E. States — Section 80-IC.

Such undertakings or enterprises which manufacture or produce any article or thing, not being those specified in the 13th Schedule, and which commence operation in any Export Processing Zone, IIDC or IGC or IE or IP or STP, etc. as notified by Board would be allowed 100% deduction of the profits of the undertaking for 10 years in the States of Sikkim and North Eastern States. For the States of Uttaranchal and Himachal Pradesh, the deduction would be 100% of the profits of the undertaking for 5 assessment years and thereafter 25% (30% for companies) for the next 5 assessment years. Similar deduction would be available to thrust sector industries as specified in he 14th Schedule as per the Finance Act, 2003 w.e.f. the A.Y. 2004-2005.

12. Tax holiday for hotel and convention centres in NCT of Delhi and other areas — Section 80ID

100% deduction of the profits and gains derived from the business of convention centres and 2-star, 3-star and 4-star category hotels in NCT of Delhi and districts of Faridabad, Gurgaon, Gautam Budh Nagar and Ghaziabad, constructed and functioning between April, 2007 and 31 march, 2010 for a five year period beginning from the initial assessment year would be allowed. This amendment is made by the Finance Act, 2007 and would be effective from the A.Y. 2008-2009

13. Deduction in respect of medical insurance premia — Section 80D

An NRI, like a resident individual is entitled to a deduction upto Rs. 15,000 in respect of medical insurance premia for health of the assessee or his spouse or dependent parents or dependent children from the A.Y. 2008-2009.

However, the deduction for medical treatment of handicapped depen-dent u/s 88DD or for terminal ailments u/s 80DDB or u/s 80U for blind persons, etc. is not allowed to NRIs as it is deductible for residents only.

14. Deduction of repayment of loan for higher studies — Section 80E

The entire amount of interest paid by an individual or his parent or spouse during the previous year on a loan for pursuing higher education taken from any financial institution or any approved charitable institution would be allowed as a deduction from the total income. However, no deduction would be allowed for repayment of the principal loan amount. This deduction would be allowed in eight years beginning from the year in which the payment of interest on loan begins. This amendment is made by the Finance Act, 2007 and is effective from the A. Y. 2008-2009.

15. Deduction in respect of certain undertakings in North Eastern States

The Finance Act, 2007 has inserted a new Section 80IE which provides for deduction from the gross total income of an assessee of an amount equal to 100% for ten Assessment Years. This benefit will be available to any undertaking which had begun or begins, for the period 1 April 2007 and ending before 1st day of April, 2017 in any of the North Eastern States of India with the following activities.

(i)   To manufacture or produce any eligible article or things;
(ii) To undertake substantial expansion to manufacture or produce any eligible article or things;
(iii) To carry on any eligible business

For the purpose of this section North Eastern States of India would mean the States of Arunachal Pradesh, Assam, Manipur, Meghalaya, Mizoram, Nagaland, Sikkim and Tripura.

This special deduction applies even in respect of substantial expansion which means increase in the investment in plant and machinery by the least twenty-five per cent of the book value of plant and machinery (before taking depreciation in any year), as on the first day of the previous year in which the substantial expansion is undertaken.

The definition of eligible article or things means the article other than the following:

(a) Goods falling under Chapter 24 of the First Schedule of the Central Excise Tariff Act, 1985, which pertains to tobacco and manufactured substitutes;

(b) Pan masala as covered under Chapter 21 of the First Schedule to the Central Excise Tariff Act, 1985;

(c) Plastic carry bags of less than 20 microns as specified by the Ministry of Environment and Forests vide Notification Number S.O. 705(E), dated 2 September 1999 and S.O. 698(E), dated 17 June 2003, and

(d) Goods falling under Chapter 27 of the First Schedule of the Central Excise Tariff Act, 1985, produced by petroleum oil or gas refineries.

Similarly, eligible business which is entitled to this deduction would mean the business of

(a) Hotel (not below two star category)

(b) Adventures and leisure sports including ropeways.

(c) Providing medical and health services in the nature of nursing home with a minimum capacity of twenty-five beds.

(d) Running an old-age home.

(e) Operating vocational training institute for hotel management, catering and food craft entrepreneurship development, nursing and para-medical, civil aviation related training, fashion designing and industrial training.

(f) Running information technology related training centre.

(g) Manufacturing of information technology hardware; and

(h) Bio-technology.

16. Other deductions like depreciation, etc. to non-resident Indians

The deductions discussed in topics 4 to 9 are deductible from the gross total income of the non-resident Indians. However, there are certain deductions and allowances which are available to a non-resident Indian while computing the gross total income itself, such as depreciation and business expenditure which is incidental to trade or industry or profession. Such deductions have not been discussed in this book as they are outside its scope. It would suffice if the non-resident Indian remembers that ordinarily all business expenditure is allowed as a deduction in the computation of profits and gains of a business unless otherwise specifically prohibited by the Income Tax Act. As most non-resident Indians have investment income, a knowledge of the various deductions under Chapter VI-A and rebate of income tax. under Chapter VIII as explained above will suffice for the purposes of enabling the non-resident Indian to compute his total income.

CHAPTER 9

Procedure for the filing of income tax and wealth tax returns, assessment, and refunds

1. Introduction

A Non-resident Indian is likely to have some income in India which may not be out of foreign exchange assets or may be such that he may like to opt for the normal assessment procedure so that he secures the advantage of a lower incidence of income tax. Under such cases, where a non-resident Indian chooses to file an income tax return or when he is required to file the income tax return, it is necessary for him or his authorised representative (known as his agent) to be familiar with the salient aspects of the assessment procedure so that he can file the return of income in time and also claim refund of income tax, if any. Likewise, he should also be familiar with other aspects of payment of advance tax and appellate procedure, etc. In this chapter we have discussed all these aspects as relevant to a non-resident Indian. The sections referred to in topics 2 to 11 of this chapter relate to the Income Tax Act 1961. In topic 15 we have discussed the salient features of the assessment procedure regarding wealth tax. A person who is liable to pay tax or is entitled to refund is known as an assessee. For the procedure regarding getting PAN, please refer to topic 15 of this chapter.

Under Section 245Q of the Income Tax Act, a non-resident can obtain an advance ruling about his tax liability in India by filing an application before the Authority for Advance Rulings, accompanied by a fee of Rs. 2,500. The Ruling is binding on the non-resident and the I.T. Department. As decided in *P.No. 25 of 1996, In re* [1999] 237 ITR 827, the applicant should be a non-resident in the previous year preceding the financial year in which the application is filed.

2. Income tax return to be voluntarily filed and tax paid on self-assessment if an NRI has taxable income in India

As stated earlier, no income tax return is to be filed by a non-resident Indian in circumstances explained in Chapter 7, topic 7. Similarly, where a non-resident Indian has in India, a total income below the taxable limit of Rs. 1,10,000 for the financial year 2007-2008, he is not required voluntarily to file an income tax return. However, an NRI may, of his own will and choice file an I.T. Return, even where the total income in India does not exceed Rs. 1,10,000. In other cases, namely, where a non-resident Indian has income exceeding the exemption limit and is not governed by the special procedure of assessment of income tax at the uniform rate of 20% he would be required to file an income tax return voluntarily. Under Section 139(1) a non-resident Indian, like any other tax payer, is required to voluntarily file his income tax return in Form No. 2 or 2D or Form No. 3, as the case may be, on or before 31st July of the assessment year concerned if he has a taxable Indian income. If the NRI is subject to tax audit, the last date for filing of I.T. Return is 31st October. For example, if a non-resident Indian has earned some business income in India for the financial year ending 31 March 2007 he can voluntarily file his return in Form No. 2 on or before 31 July 2007. Self-assessment tax under the provisions of Section 140A must be paid before filing the return of income and a copy of the challan for the self-assessment tax must be enclosed with the return. All necessary statements, challans, certificates, etc. regarding the details of the income of the non-resident must be filed along with the return of income. In case of belated return, penal interest at 1% p.m. will be levied.

The requirement of compulsory filing of an I.T. Return under the first proviso to Section 139(1) in Form No. 2C for fulfilling one of the six economic criteria viz., occupation of a property, ownership of a vehicle, credit card, etc. is not applicable to NRIs, as per Notification No.S.O.710(E) dated 20.8.1998. Now the provisions relating to compulsory filing of income tax return based on economic indicators have been deleted from the A.Y. 2006-07.

3. The Assessing Officer can also require the non-resident to file income tax return

Under the provisions of Section 139(2) an Assessing Officer may also require any assessee, including a non-resident Indian who, in his opinion had taxable income during the relevant previous year, to submit a return of income within 30 days of the receipt of such notice. Penal interest @ 12% p.a. is to be charged by the Assessing Officer for belated submission of return. The return under Section 139(1) or 139(2) can be signed by the non-resident Indian himself or by some person duly authorised by him on this behalf where the non-resident Indian is absent from India. In certain cases the return can also be filed by the agent of the non-resident Indian who is known as a representative assessee, as explained in topic 14 of this chapter.

4. NRIs can apply for refund of income tax by filing income tax return

Where the amount of income tax deductible from the income of a non-resident Indian or the amount of advance tax or any other tax paid by him or treated as paid by him or on his behalf for any assessment year exceeds the amount by which he is properly chargeable under the Income Tax Act for that year, he would be entitled to a refund of the excess income tax. Every claim for refund has to be made in the prescribed Form No. 30 obtainable from any Income tax Officer. The return of income must accompany such form. Such a claim for refund must be made within one year from the last day of the assessment year in which the income in respect of which the claim is made was assessable. Interest @ 1/2% p.m. from 1 April of the assessment year till the date the refund is granted.

5. Income of NRIs is generally accepted without scrutiny

On the receipt of an income tax return, the Assessing Officer sends an intimation, if any modification is made to the income returned. Under the new procedure the income of an individual taxpayer in about 97% of cases is normally to be accepted without scrutiny and without calling for examination of the books of accounts, etc. Hence, a non-resident Indian must exercise utmost care in filing the return of income so that it can be accepted by the Assessing Officer under Section 143(1). Thus in about 97% of the cases the acknowledgment slip serves the purpose of an assessment order under Section 143(1). In very selected cases there is a procedure of detailed scrutiny as is explained in the succeeding para. The Finance Act, 1999 had from 1.6.1999 taken away the power of the Assessing Officer to make adjustment while making a provisional assessment under Section 143(1). The Finance Act, 2001 has taken away the power of A.O. to withhold refund under Section 241.

6. Regular assessment after personal hearing, and examination of papers, etc. by the Assessing Officer

Where the Assessing Officer considers it necessary to verify the correctness and completeness of the income tax return, by requiring the presence of the assessee or the production of evidence for this purpose, the Assessing Officer must serve on the assessee (including a non-resident Indian) a notice for personal hearing or the production of evidence in support of the return under Section 143(2). This is normally done when a case is selected for detailed scrutiny on a random sampling basis. In such a case after taking into account all relevant material which the Assessing Officer has gathered and after hearing such evidence as the assessee may produce, the Assessing Officer has to make an assessment under Section 143(3). There is also a procedure for compulsory audit of accounts where the turnover, etc. exceeds Rs. 40,00,000. Most non-resident Indians may not be required to have a tax audit of their accounts, hence the provisions in this regard have not been discussed here.

7. *Ex parte* assessment by the Assessing Officer

Where the non-resident Indian fails to file the income tax return which he may be required to submit as per notice given by the Assessing Officer under Section 139(2) or where he fails to comply with all the terms of the notice issued under Section 142(1) regarding the production of accounts or a notice under Section 143(2) regarding production of evidence in support of the return of income made, the

Assessing Officer is empowered to make an assessment of the- total income of the non-resident Indian to the best of his judgement and determine the sum payable or refundable to him on the basis of such assessment. Of course, the Assessing Officer must not act dishonestly in the matter. He must make what he honestly believes to be a fair estimate of the proper figure of assessment, as explained in topic 12. An appeal against such an order and also against intimation under Section 143(1) lies with the appellate authority.

8. Re-assessment or additional assessment in case of income escaping assessment

Where the income tax chargeable has been under-assessed or where such income has been assessed at too low a rate or where excessive relief is granted to the non-resident Indian, the Assessing Officer may reassess such income or re-compute the loss for the assessment year concerned. Where the Assessing Officer believes that such assessment or re-assessment is due to the omission or failure on the part of the non-resident Indian to disclose fully and truly all facts in the return, the Assessing Officer can issue a notice under Section 148/147(a) within 4, or 6 years, depending on the quantum of income concerned.

9. Completion of assessment and payment of tax

The time limit of an assessment under Section 143(1) is a period of one year from 1 June, 2001, as per the Finance Act, 2001, and for a regular assessment under Section 143/144 it is 2 years (reduced to 21 months from the A.Y. 2004-05 by the Finance Act, 2006) from the end of the assessment year in which the income was first assessable. For example, for the assessment year 2005-2006, the Assessing Officer must complete the assessment on or before 31 December 2007. Income tax and other dues, if any, as per the notice of demand, must be paid within the time mentioned in the demand notice. Normally, a period of 30 days is allowed to an assessee for making the payment of income tax and other dues as mentioned in the notice of demand. Where it is not possible for the non-resident Indian to pay the entire tax at one time, he may make an application to the Assessing Officer to permit him to make payment of the tax in suitable instalments. Interest at 1% per month is normally required to be paid for the period of belated tax payment.

10. Provision regarding penal interest and penalty for delay in filing income tax return or payment of tax

As stated earlier, penal interest under Section 234A at 1% per month is payable by the non-resident Indian on the belated submission of the income tax return, if he is required to voluntarily submit it under the provisions of Section 139(1). Likewise, where the non-resident Indian does not furnish the return of income within 30 days, when he is required to do so through an individual notice from the Assessing Officer, penal interest at 1% p.m. is also required to be paid. Similarly, in matters of delay in payment of income tax or where the income tax is allowed to be paid by instalments, interest at 1% p.m. is normally charged from the taxpayer. Likewise, on the refund of income tax, interest at 1/2% p.m. is paid by the Central Government under Section 244A. Where there is concealment of income, the minimum penalty leviable under Section 271(1)(c) is equal to the income tax and the maximum is equal to three time the income tax sought to be evaded. For non-payment of regular income tax a penalty can be levied by the Assessing Officer under Section 221 which may be increased from time, but not as to exceed 100% of the arrear income tax.

11. Deduction of tax at source and payment of advance tax by NRIs

The income of a non-resident Indian in India in most cases is subject either to tax at source or payment of advance tax. Income by way of dividends, interest, winnings from lottery and other sums payable to non-resident Indians are subject to deduction of tax at source. Another method by which income tax payable by a non-resident Indian is collected in advance of the regular assessment is payment of advance tax. Advance tax is payable by the non-resident Indian in respect of his total income. Advance tax is payable in a financial year and is treated as a payment of tax in respect of the income of the previous year for an assessment year immediately following the financial year in which it was payable. Credit for such advance tax is given to the non-resident Indian in the regular assessment. A non-resident Indian who has been previously assessed by way of regular assessment is required to pay advance tax. Where the total income of the non-resident Indian taxable in India does not exceed Rs. 1,10,000, during the financial year 2007-2008 he is not required to pay any advance tax. Further, where the tax payable on the basis of the total income as reduced by the income tax deductible at source exceeds Rs. 5,000 the non-resident Indian would be required to pay advance tax.

Where advance tax is payable, the assessee shall himself compute the advance tax payable on his current income at the rate in force in the financial year and deposit the same whether or not he has been earlier assessed. He need not file any estimate. The Assessing Officer can also serve an order for enhanced tax based on the total income of the latest previous year for which the assessment has been made or the returned income in the latest return, whichever is higher. In such a case also the assessee shall have the right to file his own estimate for advance tax and pay tax accordingly. He may submit a revised estimate of advance tax to reduce the amount determined by the Assessing Officer. The assessee is also entitled to revise the instalment of advance tax according to his estimate of current income without the requirement of filing a revised estimate of advance tax.

Under Section 211, up to 30%, 60%, and 100% of the advance tax payable shall be paid by 15 September, 15 December, and 15 March respectively. Any payment for advance tax before 31 March will be treated as advance tax. For companies, 15%, 45%, 75% and 100% of the advance tax shall be payable by 15 June, 15 September, 15 December and 15 March.

The provisions for interest are now contained in Sections 234B and 243C. The rate of interest under Section 234B for default in payment of advance tax is 1% p.m. for the period starting from 1 April of the following financial year to the date of regular assessment on the assessed tax less advance tax, if the advance tax paid falls short of 90% of the assessed tax. Under Section 234C, the rate of interest is 1% per month in case of deferment of instalments of advance tax or at 1% on the shortfall in the payment of tax till 15 March.

The Finance Act, 2003 has, w.e.f. 1.6.2003 inserted a new Section 234D to charge simple interest on excess refund granted at the time of summary assessment at the rate of one-half per unit p.m. for the months comprised in the period from the date of grant of refund to the date of the regular assessment.

12. Remedies by way of appeal, etc. available to a non-resident Indian

The right of appeal against the order of the Assessing Officer is given only to the taxpayer and not to the Income Tax Department. Against the order of assessment or refund or any other order, the non-resident Indian can file an appeal in Form No. 35 to the Commissioner (Appeals) within 30 days of the service of notice or order against which the appeal is preferred. The minimum filing fee is Rs. 250 and the maximum Rs. 1,000. The CIT. (Appeals) will fix a date for hearing of the appeal where the non-resident Indian as well as the Assessing Officer get hearing either in person or through a representative. Normally he will pass an order within 1 year from the end of the financial year in which the appeal was filed. A further appeal against the order of the CIT (Appeals) lies with the Income Tax Appellate Tribunal. Such an appeal is to be filed in Form No. 36. The period of limitation for appeal to the Appellate Tribunal is 60 days from the date on which such an order is communicated to the assessee or CIT. The assessee is required to deposit a filing fee of Rs. 500 or Rs. 1,500 or maximum of Rs. 10,000 before preferring an appeal to the Tribunal. The order passed by the Tribunal normally within 4 years is final on questions of fact only. Against the decision of the Appellate Tribunal, a direct appeal can be filed, with a filing fee as fixed by High Court Rules on or after 1 October 1998, to the High Court of the state concerned. The period of limitation for making an appeal is 60 days. An appeal lies with the Supreme Court from a judgment of a High Court. In certain cases where the subject involved is small, a non-resident Indian can apply to the C.I.T. within one year from the date of order passed by the Assessing Officer The order of the Commissioner is final. Similarly, the C.I.T. can also revise the order of the Assessing Officer on his own, subject of course to certain conditions.

13. Other provisions for rectification and settlement of cases

A mistake apparent from record can be rectified by the authority concerned within four years from the end of the financial year in which the order sought to be rectified was passed. The authority has to pass an order under Section 154 within six months. In cases where the proposed rectification involves a debatable question, no rectification which is adverse to the assessee can be made. In certain special cases where the additional tax payable involved exceeds Rs. 1,00,000, application for the settlement of the case can be made to the Income Tax Settlement Commission.

14. Who can be an agent of a non-resident Indian?

A non-resident Indian may be assessed directly or through an agent. Section 160(1)(i) provides that "representative assessee" means in respect of the income of a non-resident, an agent including the person who is treated as an agent under Section 163. Agent of a non-resident Indian according to the provisions of Section 163 includes any person in India —

(a) who is employed by or on behalf of the non-resident Indian; or
(b) who has any business connection with non-resident; or
(c) from or through whom the non-resident is in receipt of any income whether directly or indirectly; or
(d) who is a trustee of the non-resident ; and

also includes any other person who has acquired by means of transfer a capital asset in India. No person is to be treated as an agent of a non-resident Indian unless he has had an opportunity of being heard by the Assessing Officer as to his liability to be treated as such. A non-resident Indian may also appoint an authorised representative to act as his agent. Such an agent would also be entitled to file an income tax return for and on his behalf and also for claiming refund of income tax and carry on other formalities in the matter of income tax, etc.

15. Procedure for getting a Permanent A/c Number (PAN)

A resident tax-payer having a taxable income in India has to apply for the allotment of a Permanent Account Number (PAN) as per Section 139A by making an application to his Assessing Officer in form No.49A. The application for allotment of PAN can also be made now through the Unit Trust of India. Similarly, if the total sales, turnover or gross receipts are or is likely to exceed Rs. 5 lakhs in any previous year, he must apply for the allotment of PAN. However, as per Rule 114C(1) (b), non-residents have been exempted from complying with the provisions of Section 139A regarding PAN.

16. Double Taxation Relief

The income of an NRI may sometimes be liable to tax in India as well as in the foreign country. To avoid such double taxation, the Government of India has entered into Double Taxation Avoidance (DTA) Agreements with over 70 countries as per Section 90. Hence, an NRI should refer to such DTA Agreement, if necessary. If there is no DTA Agreement of India with a foreign country and the income becomes taxable in India as well as in the foreign country then it is provided by Section 91 that unilateral relief at the lower of the two rates of tax will be given in India to a resident in India. Thus, an NRI is not entitled to such relief u/s 91.

17. Assessment procedure for wealth tax

In the preceding paras we have outlined the salient aspects of the procedure of income tax and other connected matters. The procedure of making assessment, appeal, payment of tax, etc., in the matter of wealth tax under the Wealth Tax Act 1957 in the case of a non-resident Indian broadly follows the same pattern as that under the Income Tax Act. A non-resident is liable to wealth tax in India only when the net taxable wealth in India exceeds Rs. 15 lakhs as on the valuation date. This sum of net wealth is found out after deducting all the exemptions which are described in Chapter 6. The return of net wealth is to be filed on or before the date for voluntary submission of income tax return. The rate of wealth tax is only 1% of the net wealth in excess of Rs. 15 lakh. Many items of wealth are fully exempt from wealth tax.

18. Conclusion

A non-resident Indian who is required to file a return of income or to claim refund of income tax should be familiar with the important aspects of the assessment procedure so that he does not commit any mistake in the matter of filing of income tax return or payment of tax, or claiming the refund of tax, etc. A non-resident Indian can also avoid the payment of penal interest and penalty and get proper redress by following the appellate procedure, as outlined in the preceding paras. A non-resident Indian who has income other than investment income exceeding Rs. 1,10,000 for the Assessment Year 2008-2009 must voluntarily file a return of income and be familiar with the broad aspects of the assessment procedure as described in the preceding paras. Also do remember that women NRIs must also file their income tax return only when the net taxable income exceeds Rs. 1,10,000 for the A. Y. 2008-2009. The NRI who happens to be a senior citizen must file the income tax return if his income is in excess of Rs. 1,10,000. Likewise, where the net wealth in India of a non-resident Indian exceeds Rs. 15 lakh he should voluntarily submit a return of net wealth.

CHAPTER 10

Gifts by NRIs to relatives and friends can be made fully exempt from gift tax

1. Introduction

Gift tax in India is payable by the donor, i.e. the person making the gift under the provisions of the Gift Tax Act 1958 only in respect of gift made till 30 September 1998. Gift tax was abolished on gifts made on or after 1 October 1998. This Act extends to the whole of India, except the State of Jammu and Kashmir. Likewise, this Act is also not applicable to the State of Sikkim. Gift tax is payable in respect of assessment year on the taxable gifts made by a taxpayer, i.e. the donor in a previous year relevant to the assessment year. Gift tax is payable on the total amount of all gifts made by a taxpayer during a particular previous year relevant to the assessment year concerned to one or more donees, in excess of the exemption limit and also after excluding other exemptions from gift tax. Thus gift tax is payable on the taxable gift made till 30.9.98. If a non-resident Indian knows these exemptions and makes a gift accordingly, he would not be liable to any gift tax at all under the provisions of the Gift Tax Act.

2. No aggregation of taxable gifts

Till assessment year 1986-87 there was a provision for aggregating the taxable gift made by a donor along with taxable gifts made by him during the preceding four years. The aggregated taxable gift was thus liable to gift tax at the slab rates of gift tax. From the total gift tax so payable, the gift tax, in any, paid if any of the previous years in respect of the aggregated gifts was then deducted. This provision was contained in Section 6A of the Gift Tax Act. From the assessment year 1987-88 this provision will not be applicable and thus gifts, if any, made in any previous year relevant to the assessment year 1987-88 and onwards would not be liable to aggregation of gifts. Non-resident Indians would find a great deal of relief, particularly where they make gifts in India to their relatives and friends in such a manner that they are exempt from gift tax.

3. Gift of immovable property situated outside the taxable territories is completely exempt from gift tax — regarding gift made till 30 September 1998

Under the provisions of Section 5(1)(i) of the Gift Tax Act 1958, no gift tax is to be charged in respect of all gifts made by any person till 30 September 1998 (including a non-resident Indian) of immovable property situated outside the territories to which this Act extends. As stated in topic 1, gift tax is not applicable to the State of Jammu & Kashmir and the State of Sikkim. Thus, if any non-resident Indian makes a gift of immovable property situated in Jammu & Kashmir or New York or London he would be completely exempt from payment of gift tax in respect of such gifts of immovable property. In such a case the status of the donee is immaterial, i.e. the recipient of the gift. A non-resident Indian can take full advantage of this exemption and make a gift of an immovable property situated in a foreign country or in the states of Jammu & Kashmir, and Sikkim without being liable to pay gift tax in India. If, however, a non-resident Indian makes any gift of an immovable property situated in India, he would be liable to gift tax as any other person. Gift tax is however, abolished on gifts made after 1 October 1998. This provision is explained by means of an example given below.

Illustration No. 29

C, a non-resident Indian, is an owner of a house property in London which is valued at Rs. 25,00,000. He makes a gift of the said house to his youngest son. on 8 July 2007 No gift tax would be payable in respect of the value of the house property in London gifted by C to his son.

---

4. Gifts to non-relatives by NRI is income

As per the Finance (No. 2) Act, 2004 any gift received on or after 1-9-2004 by an individual or an H.U.F. from any person including a non-resident Indian in cash or by way of credit in excess of Rs. 25,000 would be liable to tax as "Income from other sources". In the case of an individual's marriage, gifts without any upper limit even from non-relatives would be exempt. Thus, gift of jewellery, securities, property, etc. of any amount will also be exempt. Gifts received or credited by an individual from a relative out of natural love would be exempted. So also gifts received or credited by any individual or an H.U.F. under a Will or by way of inheritance or exempted sums will not be taxable as income. For the individual, "relative" would mean his spouse, brother or sister, spouse's brother or sister, parent's brother or sister, lineal ascendant or descendant of self or spouse. Spouse of these persons would also be considered as relative. In view of the above provision even the NRI should not make gifts to non-relatives keeping in view the fact that the resident non-relative would be subjected to tax thereon. As per the Taxation Laws (Amendment) Act, 2005 the gifts in cash received by an Individual or on HUF from any person other than relatives and on marriage would be exempted to the extent of Rs. 50,000 on and from the A.Y. 2007-08. The gifts from charitable trusts and institutions would, however, be exempt without any upper limit even from 1.9.2004.

5. Conclusion

The description given in this chapter of the various types of gift tax exemptions available to a non-resident Indian would prove very useful to a non-resident Indian planning gifts to his relatives or friends in India.

CHAPTER 11

FEMA and NRIs — Preliminary aspects analysed

1. Introduction

A Non-resident Indian, i.e. an NRI investing in India or having any type of business connection in India and having any income in India has not only to know the salient aspects of the Income Tax Act, 1961 but has also to be conversant with the law relating to the regulation of foreign exchange in India. The latest law in this regard is known as Foreign Exchange Management Act, 1999, which has replaced the earlier law known as FERA, 1973. The new FEMA, 1999 came into force with effect from 1.6.2000. In this chapter we have discussed certain preliminary aspects of FEMA, like the main enactment and connected Rules, Regulations, Notifications and the Reserve sank Circulars, etc. along with salient aspects of FEMA in contradistinction to FERA. The detailed aspects of FEMA as relevant for the NRIs in relation to various matters like investment in immovable property in India, making various types of deposits in India, investment in shares, units and other securities and various other investments are discussed in Chapters 12 to 18 hereinafter. In the end, we have included Chapter 19 containing FAQs (Frequently Asked Questions) on the aspects of importance for the NRIs both from the point of Income Tax Act and the FEMA. Please look for the latest up date in the Exchange Control Manual or Circulars issued by Reserve Bank of India.

2. FEMA and FERA

The Foreign Exchange Management Act, 1999 (FEMA), as mentioned earlier, has been in force with effect from 1.6.2000, thus replacing the old FERA, 1973. There is a general misunderstanding among the NRIs that all restrictions and controls relating to foreign exchange transactions have been abolished and that foreign exchange dealings would be allowed to be freely made after the enactment of FEMA. This is not so. It is, of course, true that there is a great change in the outlook of FEMA in comparison with FERA but reasonable restrictions with regard to foreign exchange transactions with a view to facilitate them in a regulated manner find a place in FEMA, 1999 and connected rules and regulations. One of the special aspects of FEMA is that various notifications and provisions of the RBI Exchange Control Manual have been reframed in the form of separate regulations for different types of exchange transactions with a view to making them available easily to NRIs and other persons and also to provide transparency to the RBI rules and regulations. For example, the various types of accounts like NR(E) Account, FCNR account, NRO Account, etc. were regulated through Exchange Control Manual and Notifications in this regard. Now, the FEMA (Deposit) Regulations deal with the maintenance and operation of such accounts in a clear cut manner. Similar is the case with reference to other various aspects of foreign exchange. The main change that the FEMA has brought in is that FEMA is a civil law, whereas the FERA was a criminal law. Under the FEMA no prosecution would be launched for contravention of operating provisions, likewise, arrest and imprisonment would not be resorted to except in the solitary case where the person, alleged to have contravened the provisions of the FEMA, defiantly resolves not to pay the penalty imposed under Section 13 of the FEMA. In the same manner unrestrained enormous powers of Directorate of Enforcement have been slashed down to a considerable extent. Even the word "offence" is conspicuous by its absence in the substantive provisions of FEMA. There are 49 sections in all in FEMA. Of these, only seven sections, namely, Sections 3 to 9 deal with certain acts to be done or not to be done in connection with transactions involving foreign exchange, foreign security, etc. There are various sections from 16 to 35 relating only to adjudication and appeal. Further, one of the most important and distinguishing features of FEMA is that there is a provision for compounding of penalty as contained in Section 15 of FEMA. This could not have been imagined earlier under FERA. Thus, NRIs and residents will have much easier time under FEMA.

3. NRIs under Income Tax Act and persons resident outside India under FEMA

The expression Non-resident Indian or an NRI is used both under the Income Tax Act and FEMA. However, there is a great difference between the meaning of both the expressions. Sometimes, a person may be NRI under the I.T. Act but he may not NRI under the FEMA or vice versa. This is because NRI, i.e., an Indian Resident outside India under

FEMA is treated differently now than he used to be under FERA. As regards the definition of the expression "Non-resident" under the I.T. Act reference may be made to Chapter 1. The expression used under FEMA is "person resident outside India". Thus, Section 2(w) of FEMA defines a "person resident outside India" as a person who is not a resident in India. Hence, it becomes very important for us to know the meaning of the expression "a person resident in India". As per Section 2(v) of FEMA a person resident in India means —

(i) a person residing in India for more than one hundred and eighty-two days during the course of the preceding financial year but does not include—

  (A) a person who has gone out of India or who stays outside India, in either case—
  (a) for or on taking up employment outside India, or
  (b) for carrying on outside India a business or vocation outside India, or
  (c) for any other purpose, in such circumstances as would indicate his intention to stay outside India for an uncertain period;

  (B) a person who has come to or stays in India, in either case, otherwise than —
  (a) for or on taking up employment in India, or
  (b) for carrying on in India a business or vocation in India, or
  (c) for any other purpose, in such circumstances as would indicate his intention to stay in India for an uncertain period;

(ii) any person or body corporate registered or incorporated in India,

(iii) an office, branch or agency in India owned or controlled by a person resident outside India,

(iv) an office, branch or agency outside India owned or controlled by a person resident in India.

Thus, the residential status of a person under FEMA depends on his residential status in the preceding financial year. Thus, Section 2(v) (i) incorporates the text of a person having resided in India for more than 182 days during the preceding financial year. Hence, a person would be deemed to be a resident of India, if he goes abroad but without taking up the employment or without carrying on business or vocation outside

India. Likewise, if a person who was resident in India, for more than 182 days in the preceding financial year goes abroad to stay with his relatives, he would continue to be a resident of India unless he obtains a "permanent resident visa or a citizenship of a foreign country". For conclusive proof that a person is a resident outside India under FEMA, he should take up employment outside India or carry on outside India any person or profession or vocation. An Indian citizen who is a Non-resident as per the definition of Section 2(w), i.e. who does not come under the definition of "Person Resident in India" as per Section 2(v) of FEMA is an NRI and will also include a Non-resident person of Indian origin. Persons of Indian Origin (PIO) Card Scheme was launched on 31st March, 1999 for conferring advantage to an estimated 15 million PIOs. Persons of Indian Origin settled in countries other than Pakistan, and Bangladesh will be issued PIO cards that would exempt them from the requirement of a visa to visit India. This scheme treats them on par with other NRIs in respect of facilities under FEMA. A PIO Card is valid for a period of twenty years subject to validity of the passport of the applicant. The persons eligible for issuance of PIO Cards would include the persons who at any time held an Indian passport, or either of grand parents or great grand parents were born in and permanently resident in India or who is a spouse of a citizen of India or a PIO as mentioned earlier. Generally speaking, the expression NRI under the I.T. Act and Persons Outside India or NRI under the FEMA are used interchangeably but the distinction based on a number of days in the preceding year under the current year under the FEMA and the I.T. Act as explained in Chapter I and above should be noted very carefully by every NRI.

4. FEMA Rules

The Foreign Exchange Management Act, 1999 (FEMA) contains only the substantive and procedural aspects of Foreign Exchange Regulations. The detailed provisions in regard to various aspects connected with Foreign Exchange Regulations are found in Rules, Regulations and Notifications under FEMA issued or promulgated by the Government of India or RBI. Thus, the Government of India, in exercise of the powers conferred on it under Section 46 of FEMA, has made various sets of Rules, namely—

4.1 Foreign Exchange Management (Current Transactions) Rules, 2000.
4.2 Foreign Exchange (Compounding Proceedings) Rules, 2000.
4.3 Foreign Exchange Management (Adjudication Proceedings and Appeal), Rules, 2000.

4.4 Foreign Exchange (Authentication of Documents) Rules, 2000.

4.5 Foreign Exchange Management (Encashment of Draft, Cheque Instrument and Payment of Interest) Rules, 2000.

FEMA came into force from 1.6.2000. Some of the most important Rules as given in detail in the different Regulations have been explained in the following Chapters from 12 to 18 of this book.

5. RBI Regulations under FEMA

Section 47 of FEMA empowers the Reserve Bank of India to make regulations to carry out the provisions of the FEMA, and the rules made thereunder. In pursuance thereto, the RBI has made the following 21 regulations so far, dealing with different types of transactions involving foreign exchange, viz.—

1. Foreign Exchange Management (Permissible Capital Account Transactions) Regulations, 2000
2. Foreign Exchange Management (Issue of Security in India by a Branch, Office or Agency of a Person Resident Outside India) Regulations, 2000
3. Foreign Exchange Management (Borrowings or Lending in Foreign Exchange) Regulations, 2000
4. Foreign Exchange Management (Borrowing and Lending in Rupees) Regulations, 2000
5. Foreign Exchange Management (Deposit) Regulations, 2000
6   Foreign Exchange Management (Acquisition and Transfer of Immovable Property Outside India) Regulations, 2000
7. Foreign Exchange Management (Guarantees) Regulations, 2000
8. Foreign Exchange Management (Insurance) Regulations, 2000
9. Foreign Exchange Management (Remittance of Assets) Regulations, 2000
10. Foreign Exchange Management (Acquisition and Transfer of Immovable Property in India) Regulations, 2000
11. Foreign Exchange Management (Establishment in India or Branch or Office or other Place of Business) Regulations, 2000
12. Foreign Exchange Management (Investment in Firm or Proprietary Concern in India) Regulations, 2000
13. Foreign Exchange Management (Export and Import of Currency) Regulations, 2000
14. Foreign Exchange Management (Transfer or Issue of any Foreign Security) Regulations 2000
15. Foreign Exchange Management (Transfer or Issue of Security by a Person Resident outside India) Regulations, 2000

16. Foreign Exchange Management (Export of Goods and Services) Regulations, 2000
17. Foreign Exchange Management (Realisation, Repatriation and Surrender of Foreign Exchange) Regulations, 2000
18. Foreign Exchange Management (Foreign Currency Accounts by a Person Resident in India) Regulations, 2000
19. Foreign Exchange Management (Possession and Retention of Foreign Currency) Regulations, 2000
20. Foreign Exchange Management (Manner of Receipt and Payment) Regulations, 2000
21. Foreign Exchange Management (Foreign Exchange Derivative Contracts) Regulations, 2000

Some of the important Regulations of great relevance for NRIs in general have been explained in detail in Chapters 12 to 18. The relevant Regulation number along with the Schedule and Annexure has also been given in the following chapters, wherever necessary.

6. Notifications

The Central Government has also notified various other matters through its notifications concerning, say Appointment of Chairperson and Members of Appellate Tribunal, Appointment of Officers of Enforcement. Likewise, a Notification No. FEMA 17/2000-RB, dated 3.5.2000 relaxes the transactions with Nepal and Bhutan by directing that the prohibitions imposed by clauses (b), (c), and (d) of Section 3 of FEMA shall not apply to any transaction entered into in Indian rupees by or with:

(i) a person who is a citizen of India, Nepal or Bhutan resident in Nepal or Bhutan;
(ii) a branch situated in Nepal or Bhutan of any business carried on by a company or a corporation incorporated under any law in force in India, Nepal or Bhutan;
(iii) a branch situated in Nepal or Bhutan of any business carried on as a partnership firm or otherwise, by a citizen of India, Nepal or Bhutan. This Notification has also come into effect from 1.6.2000.

7. RBI guidelines

The RBI has also issued directions and guidelines through its circulars issued under FEMA. For example, the RBI vide its Circular No. AD(MA Series) Circular No.11 dated 16th May, 2000 has issued various clarifications on new Rules and Regulations framed under FEMA. One of the important clarification is that pending issue of further instructions authorised dealers may be guided by the existing provisions of the

Exchange Control Manual referred to in "Annexure V" as also other Annexures of the said Circular of the RBI. The said Annexure V is reproduced below for the benefit of NRIs as they can refer to various matters covered by the Exchange Control Manual in this regard.

Pending issue of further directions authorised dealers may be guided by the following provisions of the Exchange Control Manual

Chapter	Paragraph No.	Subject matter
1.	1.4	Authorised dealers in foreign exchange
	1.5	Authorised Co-operative/Commercial Banks (These banks will now be permitted to also maintain NRSR Accounts.)
	1.6	Authorised Money Changers
	1.7	Revocation of licences/authorisation granted by Reserve Bank
	1.16	Marking of documents
	1.17	Organisation of Exchange Control Department
	1.22	Breach of regulations by non-residents branches/correspondents of authorised dealers
	1.24	Employment of Brokers
3.	3A.1	Purchase of TTs, MTs, etc. from Public
	3A.5	Foreign Inward remittance Payment System (This has been withdrawn vide Cir. No. 78, dt. 13.3.2004)
	3A.6	Issue of bank certificates
	3A.7	Refund of inward remittance
	3B.3(i)	Procedure for making applications
	3B.3(iii)	-do-
	3B.5	Manner of payment of rupees against sale of foreign exchange.
	3B.10	Undertaking/Certificate regarding payment of Income-tax
	3D.2	Purchases from Public
	3D.3	Purchases against Currency Declaration Form
	3D.4	Encashment Certificates
	3D.5	Purchases on Authorised Dealer's own responsibility
	3D.6	Import of Foreign Currency notes
	3D.8	Reconversion of Indian currency
	3D.9	Sales to Foreign Tourists
	3D.9A	Providing Foreign Currency Travellers Cheques and notes to the Master/Captain of foreign vessels against inward remittance
	3D.11	Sales to other authorised dealers, Exchange Bureaux and Money Changers
	3D.12	Rates of Exchange
	3D.13	Display of exchange rates

Contd...

Chapter	Paragraph No.	Subject matter
	3D.14	Regulation of authorised dealers' sales to travellers
	3D.15	Export of surplus currency notes and coins
	3D.16	Records to be maintained by Exchange Bureaux
	3D.17	Reporting of transactions by Exchange Bureaux
4.	4.1 to 4.8	Provisions relating to authorised dealers' dealings with Reserve Bank
5.	Part A 5A.I to 5A.11	Rupee accounts of non-resident banks
	Part B 5B.I to 5B.6	Inter-bank dealings
	Annexure	Guidelines for foreign exchange exposure limits to authorised dealers
7.	7A.1(i) and (ii)	General
	7A.2	Import licences
	7A.4	Manner of rupee payment
	7A.5	Letter of authority
	7A.6	Attestation of invoices by authorised dealers
	7A.7	Form A1
	7A.8	Imports financed in rupees
	7A.9	Import licence for CIF value
	7A.9A	Imports by Government/Public Sector Undertakings, etc.
	7A.10	Advance Remittance (except that amount of US $ 15,000 or its equivalent may be amended as US $ 25,000 or its equivalent)
	7A.11	Time limit for settlement of import payments
	7A.12	Interest on import bills
	7A.15	Endorsement on Import Licences
	7A.20	Evidence of imports
	7A.21	Precautions for handling import documents
8.	8A.1(d)	Sale of exchange — Endorsement on passport
	8A.1(e)	Issue of Travellers Cheques
	8A.1(f)	Sale of exchange in the form of foreign currency notes
	8A.1(g)	Retention of Form A2
	8A.3(ii)	Endorsement of unspent exchange on the passport
	8A.9	Remittance for tour arrangement] (The paras 7 and 8 of ECM are no longer applicable now; hence they stand suspended)
16.	16.1 to 16.9	Returns and Statements (including Guide to authorised dealers for compilation of 'R' returns).

8. Foreign investments in India

Liberalisation measures have been introduced with regard to foreign investments in India vide RBI Circular No. 38 dated 3-12-2003. For details refer to Reserve Bank of India's web site www.ecm.rbi.org.in and fema.rbi.org.in. For clarifications e-mail at rbndinfo@vsnl.com

Acquisition and transfer of immovable property in India by NRIs and FEMA

1. Introduction

Detailed provisions have been made in the FEMA as also in the Rules and Regulations made thereunder about the acquisition or transfer of immovable property in India by a person resident outside India including an NRI. Hence, it is necessary to go through these provisions. The general rule is that liberal permission has been granted for the NRIs to acquire and transfer an immovable property in India. However, a distinction is based on citizenship of India between NRIs who are Indian citizens and NRIs of Indian origin. In some cases, other Non-residents also are permitted to acquire an immovable property in India subject to certain conditions. Thus, the general rule is that unless it is permitted under the FEMA or under its Rules and Regulations, the acquisition or transfer of an immovable property in India by a person including an Indian citizen resident outside India would require an approval from the Reserve Bank of India vide Notification No. FEMA-21/2000-RB dated 3.5.2000. A Notification has been issued by the Reserve Bank of India in this regard and is known as Foreign Exchange Management (Acquisition and Transfer of Immovable Property in India) Regulations, 2000. This is modified by RBI Circular No. 43 dated 8-12-2003. The salient features of these Regulations are given in this and other chapters. For the latest relaxation in these Regulations, please enquire from the Reserve Bank of India.

2. NRIs can hold, own or transfer immovable property in India without any condition

Under Section 6(5) of FEMA, a person resident outside India can hold, own or transfer immovable property in India if such property is acquired by him when he was a resident in India or inherited from a person resident in India. Thus, this provision facilitates the ownership and transfer of immovable property in India by former residents and there is no impediment to their continuing to hold such property or transfer such property even when they become NRI. However, an NRI should be very cautious in dealing with reputed builders or agents only. If there is a proposal for joint investment, he should make sure that the money reaches the right person only. He should also ascertain the exact contribution and the extent of ownership in joint investments.

3. Acquisition and transfer of immovable property by an NRI

In terms of Regulation No.3 of the aforesaid Regulations, an Indian citizen resident outside India is permitted to —

(a) acquire any immovable property in India other than agricultural/plantation property or a farm house;
(b) transfer any property in India to a person resident in India;
(c) transfer any property other than agricultural or plantation property or a farm house to an Indian citizen or a person of Indian origin as defined in Regulation 2(c), resident outside India.

NRIs who are Indian citizens enjoy great privileges in the matter of acquisition and transfer of an immovable property in India as mentioned above. This privilege is not enjoyed by a Non-resident person of Indian origin, namely, a Non-resident who is not a citizen of India. For him, this provision is described in topic 4 below.

4. Acquisition and transfer of an immovable property by a person of Indian origin

Regulation No.4 of the aforesaid Regulations permits a person of Indian origin to:

(a) acquire immovable property other than agricultural land/plantation property or a farm house by way of purchase subject to the conditions regarding RBI rules mentioned in clause (a) of the Regulation;
(b) acquire any immovable property other than agricultural land/plantation property/farm house by way of gift from an Indian citizen resident outside India or from a PIO;

(c) acquire property by inheritance subject to the conditions stipulated in clause (c) of the Regulation;

(d) transfer by way of sale any immovable property other than agricultural/plantation property or a farm house by way of sale to a person resident in India;

(e) transfer agricultural land/farm house or plantation property way of gift or sale to an Indian citizen resident in India.

(f) transfer residential or commercial property in India by way of gift to a person resident in India or to a person resident outside India who is a citizen of India or to a person of Indian origin resident outside India.

5. Acquisition of immovable property for permitted activity

A person resident outside India who has established in India in accordance with the Foreign Exchange Management (Establishment in India of a Branch or Office or Other Place of Business) Regulations, 2000, a branch office or other place of business for carrying on in India any activity, excluding a liaison office has been permitted to acquire immovable property in India which is necessary for or incidental to the activity carried on in India by such branch or office subject to the terms and conditions mentioned in Regulation No.5, reproduced in topic 8 below. Such property can also be mortgaged to an authorised dealer as a security for any borrowing by a branch or office. However, a declaration in Form No.IPI has to be filed in duplicate and submitted directly to the Chief General Manager, Exchange Control Department, (Foreign Investment Division-II), Reserve Bank of India, Central Office, Bombay-400001 within 90 days from the date of acquisition of the said immovable property.

6. Repatriation of Sale Proceeds

Authorised dealers have been permitted to allow remittance of sales proceeds of property other than agricultural/plantation property or a farm house to an Indian citizen resident outside India or a PIO as defined in clause (c) of Regulation No.2 (See Chapter 11, topic 3), who has sold the property in India subject to terms and conditions stipulated in Regulation No.6. The important condition in this regard is that the sale should take place after three years from the date of acquisition of such immovable property or from the date of the payment of final instalment of consideration for its acquisition, whichever is later. In the case of residential property, repatriation of sale proceeds is restricted to not more than two such properties. Another condition about the repatriation of the amount is that such amount should not exceed (a) the amount paid for the acquisition of the immovable property in foreign exchange received through normal banking channels, or out of fund held in Foreign Currency Non-resident Account, or (b) the foreign currency equivalent, as on the date of payment, of the amount paid where such payment was made from the funds held in Non-resident External Account for acquisition of the property.

7. Prohibition on acquisition or transfer of immovable property in India by citizens of certain countries

A person who is a citizen of Pakistan, Bangladesh, Sri Lanka, Afghanistan, China, Iran, Nepal or Bhutan requires approval of Reserve Bank for acquisition of transfer of property in India other than lease not exceeding 5 years, in terms of Regulation No.7.

8. Latest amendments regarding acquisition of immovable properties

Vide Circular No. 43 dated 8-12-2003 the Foreign Exchange Management (Acquisition and Transfer of Immovable Property in India) Regulations 2000 has been amended. The summary with regard to the provisions relating to liberalisation of acquisition and transfer of immovable property by foreign companies and persons resident outside India is as under:—

FOREIGN INVESTMENTS IN INDIA — A SUMMARY OF UPDATED INSTRUCTIONS REGARDING ACQUISITION OF IMMOVABLE PROPERTY

Acquisition and Transfer of Immovable Property in India

1(i). *Acquisition by a person resident outside India* - A person resident outside India who is a citizen of India can acquire any immovable property in India other than agricultural/plantation/farm house.

(ii). *Acquisition by way of transfer* - A person resident outside India may transfer any immovable property other than agricultural or plantation property or farm house to a person resident outside India who is a citizen of India or to a person of Indian origin (PIO) resident outside India or a person resident in India. He may however transfer agricultural land/plantation property/farm house in India other than agricultural permanently residing in India. A PIO can transfer any immovable property in India other than agricultural land/farm house/plantation property by way of sale to a person resident in India and agricultural land/plantation/farm house by way of gift or sale to only an Indian citizen permanently residing in India. He may also transfer residential or commercial property in India by way of gift to a person resident in India or to a person resident outside India who is a citizen of India or to a person of Indian origin resident outside India.

(iii) *Acquisition by way of Gift* - A PIO resident outside India can acquire any immovable property other than agricultural land/farm house/ plantation property in India by purchase or by way of gift and any immovable property by way of inheritance. For acquiring the property, the funds should come from abroad or by debit to any non-resident account, viz., NRE/FCNR/NRO account of the investor. The gift can be received from a person resident in India or from a person resident outside India who is a citizen of India or from a PIO resident outside India.

(iv) *Acquisition by way of inheritance* - The immovable property can be acquired by PIO by way of inheritance from a person resident in India or a person resident outside India provided he has in turn acquired such property in accordance with Foreign Exchange Law/Regulations in force at the time of acquisition.

Purchase/Sale of Immovable Property by Foreign Embassies/Diplomats/Consulate Generals

2. Foreign Embassy/Diplomat/Consulate General has been allowed to purchase/sell immovable property in India other than agricultural land/plantation property/farm house provided (i) clearance from Government of India, Ministry of External Affairs is obtained for such purchase/sale, and (ii) the consideration for acquisition of immovable property in India is paid out of funds remitted from abroad through banking channel.

Acquisition of Immovable Property for carrying on a permitted activity

3. A person resident outside India who has a branch, office or other place of business (excluding a liaison office) for carrying on his business activity with requisite approvals in India may acquire an immovable property in India which is necessary for or incidental to carrying on such activity provided that all applicable laws, rules, regulations or directions for the time being in force are duly complied with. The entity/concerned person would have to file a declaration in form IPI with the Reserve Bank, within ninety days from the date of such acquisition. The non-resident is eligible to transfer by way of mortgage the said immovable property to an Authorised Dealer as a security for any borrowing.

Repatriation of sale proceeds

4. In the event of sale of immovable property other than agricultural land/farm house/plantation property in India, Authorised Dealer may allow repatriation of sale proceeds outside India provided;

(i) The immovable property was acquired by the seller in accordance with the provisions of he Foreign Exchange Law in force at the time of acquisition by him or the provisions of FEMA Regulations;

(ii) The amount to be repatriated does not exceed (a) the amount paid for acquisition of the immovable property in foreign exchange received through normal banking channels or out of funds held in Foreign Currency Non-Resident Account or (b) the foreign currency equivalent as on the date of payment of the amount paid where such payment was made from the funds held in Non-Resident External Account for acquisition of the property.

(iii) In the case of residential property, the repatriation of sale proceeds is restricted to not more than two such properties.

(iv) Authorised Dealers may allow to NRIs/PIOs the facility of repatriation of funds out of balances held in their Non-resident Rupee (NRO) Accounts upto USD one million per calendar year, including sale proceeds of immovable property, subject to production of an undertaking by the remitter and a certificate by a Chartered Accountant in the formats prescribed by the Central Board of Direct Taxes (CBDT) (enclosed to A.P. (DIR Series) Circular No. 56 dated November 26, 2002).

Prohibition on acquisition or transfer of immovable property in India by citizens of certain countries

5. No person being a citizen of Pakistan, Bangladesh, Sri Lanka, Afghanistan, China, Iran, Nepal or Bhutan shall acquire or transfer immovable property in India, other than on lease, not exceeding five years, without prior permission of the Reserve Bank.

Amendment of the Regulations (Vide Notification No. FEMA. 93/2003-RB dated June 9, 2003)

In the Foreign Exchange Management (Acquisition and Transfer of Immovable Property in India) Regulations 2000, after Regulation 5, the following Regulation shall be inserted namely:

"5A. Purchase/sale of Immovable Property by Foreign Embassies/Diplomats/Consulate Generals

A Foreign Embassy/Diplomat/Consulate General may purchase/sell immovable property in India other than agricultural land/plantation property/farm house provided (i) clearance from Government of India, Ministry of External Affairs is obtained for such purchase/sale, and (ii) the consideration for acquisition of immovable property in India is paid out of funds remitted from abroad through banking channel".

These have been amended by RBI Master Circular No. 5/2005-06 dt. 1.7.2005. A PIO may transfer agricultural land / plantation property/ farmhouse in India by way of sale or gift to person resident in India who is a citizen of India.

CHAPTER 13

Permissible and prohibited current account transactions

1. Introduction

Section 5 of the FEMA provides that any person may sell or draw foreign exchange to or from an authorised person if such sale or drawal is a current account transaction. However, the proviso to Section 5 provides that the Central Government may, in public interest and in consultation with the Reserve Bank, impose such reasonable restrictions for current account transaction as may be prescribed. The expression "current account transaction" as per Section 2(j) of FEMA is defined as under:

> 2(j) "current account transaction" means a transaction other than a capital account transaction and without prejudice to the generality of the foregoing such transaction includes, —
>
> (i) payments due in connection with foreign trade, other current business, services, and short-term banking and credit facilities in the ordinary course of business,
>
> (ii) payments due as interest on loans and as net income from investments,
>
> (iii) remittances for living expenses of parents, spouse and children residing abroad, and
>
> (iv) expenses in connection with foreign travel, education and medical care of parents, spouse and children.

Hence, the Government of India have accordingly issued a Notification No. GSR 381(E) dated 3.5.2000 notifying the Foreign Exchange Management (Current Account Transactions) Rules, 2000 in terms of which drawal of exchange for certain transactions has been prohibited and restrictions have been placed on certain transactions.

These are given in topic 2 below.

2. Prohibited categories of current account transactions

In terms of Rule 3 of the aforesaid Rules, drawal of exchange for the following transactions is prohibited:

(i)   Travel to Nepal or Bhutan.
(ii)   Transactions with a person resident in Nepal or Bhutan (unless specifically exempted by Reserve Bank by general or special order).
(iii)   Remittance out of lottery winnings.
(iv)   Remittance of income from racing/riding etc., or any other hobby.
(v)   Remittance for purchases of lottery tickets, banned/prescribed magazines, football pools, sweepstakes, etc.
(vi)   Payment of commission on exports made towards equity investment in Joint Ventures/Wholly Owned Subsidiaries abroad of Indian companies.
(vii)   Remittance of dividend by any company to which the requirement of dividend balancing is applicable.
(viii) Payment of commission on exports under Rupee State Credit Route.
(ix)   Payment related to "Call Back Services" of telephones,
(x)   Remittance of interest income on funds held in Non-Resident Special Rupee(NRSR) account scheme.

Detailed provisions can be seen in Schedule 1 annexed to the aforesaid Rules.

3. Prior approval of Government of India required for certain transactions

There are certain transactions which are included in Schedule II to the Rules, in respect of which Rule 4 of the aforesaid Rules provide that prior approval of the Government of India is required for remittance of such Current Account Transactions. Such items include cultural tours, advertisements, hiring charges of transponders, membership of P&I Club, etc. However, Rule 4 does not apply where the payment is made out of funds held in RFC Account or EEFC Account of the remitter.

4. Prior approval of Reserve Bank required for certain current account transactions

Rule 5 of the aforesaid Rules provide that no person shall draw foreign exchange for a transaction included in the Schedule III without prior approval of the Reserve Bank. This Schedule has been given below in topic 5. There are various monetary limits laid down for certain items like gift remittance exceeding US$ 5,000 per beneficiary per annum, donation exceeding US$ 5,000 per annum per beneficiary, etc. However, it is provided that this Rule does not apply where the payment is made out of funds held in RFC Account or EEFC Account of the remitter. Resident individuals can acquire foreign exchange up to $ 10,000 per calendar year for their overseas travel except for visits to Nepal and Bhutan. For the latest relaxations please contact the Reserve Bank of India.

5. Liberalisation of current account transactions

Vide RBI circular No. 76 dated 24-2-2004 provisions relating to current account transactions have been liberalised. The following is the extract of the circular:

1. Attention of Authorised Dealers (ADs) is invited to Annexure I of A.D. (M.A. Series) Circular No. 11 dated May 16, 2000 with regard to Rules relating to Current Account Transactions.
2. As a step towards further liberalisation, it has been decided to remove the following restrictions on remittances by residents.

(i) Remittance for securing Insurance for Health from a Company Abroad

In terms of item No. 10 of Schedule II, payment for securing insurance for health from a company abroad requires the approval of Ministry of Finance (Insurance Division). It has since been decided that Government's approval would not be required and Authorised Dealers (ADs) may freely allow such remittances.

(ii) Remittance by Artiste

In terms of item No. 11 of Schedule III, remittance by artistes e.g. wrestler, dancer, entertainer, etc., requires prior approval of RBI. Henceforth, ADs may freely allow such remittances.

(iii) Commission to Agents abroad for Sale of Residential Flats/Commercial Plots in India

In terms of item No. 11 of Schedule III, remittance by way of commission to agents abroad for sale of residential flats/commercial plots in India, exceeding 5 per cent of the inward remittance requires RBI's approval. ADs may freely allow such remittances upto USD 25,000 or 5 per cent of the inward remittance, per transaction, whichever is higher.

(iv) Short-term Credit to Overseas Offices of Indian Companies

In terms of item No. 12 of Schedule III, short term credit to overseas offices of Indian companies requires prior approval of RBI. Henceforth, ADs may allow such facility without RBI's approval.

(v) Remittance for Advertisement on Foreign Television Channels

In terms of item No. 13 of Schedule III, RBI's prior approval is required in cases where the export earnings of the advertiser are less than Rs. 10 lakhs during each of the preceding 2 years. Henceforth, ADs may freely allow remittances for advertisement on foreign television channels.

(vi) Remittance of Royalty and Payment of lump sum fee

In terms of item No.14 of Schedule III, RBI's prior approval is required if the agreement for technical collaboration has not been registered with RBI. Henceforth, ADs may allow remittances for royalty and payment of lump sum fee provided the payments are in conformity with the norms as per item No. 8 of Schedule II i.e. royalty does not exceed 5 per cent on local sales and 8 per cent on exports and lump sum payment does not exceed USD 2 million.

(vii) Remittance for Use and/or Purchase of Trademark/Franchise in India

In terms of item No. 16 of Schedule III, RBI's prior approval is required for remittance towards use and/or purchase of trademark/franchise in India. Henceforth, ADs may freely allow remittances for use of trade mark/franchise in India. However, RBI's prior approval will continue to be required for remittance towards purchase of trademark/franchise.

(viii) Remittance of Hiring Charges of Transponders

In terms of item No. 18 of Schedule III, RBI's prior approval is required for remittance of hiring charges of transponders. This item stands shifted to Schedule II of the Foreign Exchange Management (Current Account Transaction) Rules, 2000 and henceforth, the proposal for hiring of transponders by TV Channels and internet service providers will require prior approval of the Ministry of Information & Broadcasting.

3. Necessary amendments to the Foreign Exchange Management (Current Account Transactions) Rules, 2000 are being notified separately.

4. Authorised Dealers may bring the contents of this circular to the notice of their constituents concerned.

5. The directions contained in this circular have been issued under Section 10(4) and 11(1) of the Foreign Exchange Management Act, 1999 (42 of 1999).

Reference may also be made to RBI's AP (DIR Series) Circular No. 64, dt. 4.2.2004, No. 80 dt. 18.3.2004 and No. 38 dt. 31.3.2005 as there is a Liberalised Remittance Scheme of US $25,000 per calendar year for any permissible current account or capital account transactions or a combination of both.

Besides, Resident Indians going abroad for employment can acquire foreign exchange up to $1,00,000. Similarly, for medical treatment outside India, a resident individual can obtain foreign exchange up to $ 1,00,000 by giving a self-declaration. Students can acquire foreign exchange up to $ 1,00,000 per academic year for meeting their tuition and other costs in respect of their studies overseas. This can be obtained from the authorized dealers. Unspent foreign exchange has to be surrendered within 90 days from the date of return of the traveller. For traveller's cheques it is 180 days. However, upto $ 2,000 can be retained for subsequent travels.

CHAPTER 14

Permissible capital account transactions

1. Introduction

Under Section 6(2) of FEMA the Reserve Bank has been permitted, in consultation with the Central Government to specify any class or classes of Capital Account Transactions which are permissible and the limit upto which the foreign exchange would be admissible for such transactions. However, it is also provided that the Reserve Bank would not impose any restriction on drawal of foreign exchange for payment due on account of amortisation of loans or for depreciation of direct investment in the ordinary course of various business matters relating to Foreign Exchange Capital Transactions have been specified in Section 6(3) of FEMA. Under these powers the Reserve Bank had notified Foreign Exchange Management (Permissible Capital Account Transactions) Regulations, 2000 effective from 1.6.2000 by RBI Notification No. FEMA 1/2000-RB dated 3.5.2000. It was also provided by Section 6(4) of FEMA that a person resident in India may hold, own, transfer or invest in foreign currency, foreign security or any immovable property situated outside India if such currency, security or property was acquired, held, or owned by such person when he was resident outside India or inherited from a person who was resident outside India. A person resident in India may hold, own, transfer or invest in Indian currency, security or any immovable property situated in India if such currency, security, or property was acquired, held, or owned by such person when he was resident in India or inherited from a person who was resident in India, as laid down in Section 6 (5) of FEMA.

In terms of Foreign Exchange Management (Permissible Capital Account Transactions) Regulations, 2000 investment in India by a person resident outside India in any company or partnership firm or proprietary concern which is engaged in the business of chit fund or as a Nidhi Company, or in agricultural or plantation activities, or in real estate business (other than development of townships, construction of residential/commercial premises, roads or bridges), or construction of farm houses, in trading in Transferable Development Rights is prohibited. The expression "Transferable Development Rights" as per Regulation 2(d) of the aforesaid Regulations means certificate issued in respect of category of land acquired for public purpose either by Central or State Government in consideration of surrender of land by the owner without monetary compensation, which are transferable in part or whole. Hence, every NRI should know the permissible and the prohibited Capital Account Transactions so that he may not commit error in the matter of carrying out Capital Account Transactions in foreign exchange.

For the latest relaxations please contact the Reserve Bank of India.

2. Permissible capital account transactions

As per Regulation 3, capital account transactions of a person have been classified into two heads, namely transactions, specified in Schedule I, of a person resident in India, and transactions, specified in Schedule II, of a person resident outside India. It has also been laid down in this Regulation subject to the provisions of the FEMA or the rules or regulations or direction or orders made or issued thereunder, any person may sell or draw foreign exchange to or from an authorised person for a capital account transaction specified in the Schedules I and II. However, the transaction should be within the limit, if any, specified in the regulations relevant to the said transaction. Thus, Schedule I of the aforesaid Resolution contains the classes of capital account transactions of persons resident in India. Broadly speaking, they relate to investment by a person resident in India in foreign securities, foreign currency loans raised in India and abroad, transfer of immovable property outside India, guarantees issued by a person resident in India. In favour of a person resident outside India, export, import and holding of currency/currency notes, loans and overdrafts (borrowing) from a person outside India, maintenance of foreign currency accounts in India and outside India, taking out of insurance policy from an insurance company outside India, loans and overdrafts to a person resident outside India, remittance, outside India of capital assets, and sale and purchase of foreign exchange derivatives in India and abroad and commodity derivatives abroad. All these matters pertain to a person resident in India. For the aforesaid matters various Regulations have been notified by the Reserve Bank separately. For example, the important Regulations in this connection are:—

(1) Foreign Exchange Management (Transfer or issue of any Foreign Security) Regulations, 2000 superceded in 2004.

(2) Foreign Exchange Management (Borrowing or Lending in Foreign Exchange) Regulations, 2000.

(3) Foreign Exchange Management (Acquisition and Transfer of Immovable Property Outside India) Regulations, 2000.

(4) Foreign Exchange Management (Guarantees) Regulations, 2000.

(5) Foreign Exchange Management (Export and import of Currency) Regulations, 2000.

(6) Foreign Exchange Management (Borrowing and Lending in Rupees) Regulations, 2000.

(7) Foreign Exchange Management (Foreign Currency Accounts by a Person Resident in India) Regulations, 2000.

(8) Foreign Exchange Management (Insurance) Regulations, 2000.

(9) Foreign Exchange Management (Foreign Exchange Derivative Contracts) Regulations, 2000.

3. Classes of capital account transactions of persons resident outside India

In terms of Regulation 3(1) (B) of Foreign Exchange Management (Permissible Capital Account Transactions) Regulation, 2000, as referred to above, seven different types of classes have been laid down in Schedule II. These pertain to the capital account transactions in foreign exchange of persons who are resident outside India, i.e. concerning the NRIs as such. These relate to investment in India by the issue of security by a body corporate or an entity in India and investment therein and investment by way of contribution to the capital of a firm or a proprietorship concern or an association of persons in India, acquisition and transfer of immovable property in India, guarantee by a person in favour of, or on behalf of a person resident in India, import and export of currency/currency notes into/from India, deposits between a person resident in India and a person resident outside India, foreign currency accounts in India and remittance outside India of capital assets in India. All these matters pertain to the capital account transactions of persons who are resident outside India. The various Regulations notified by the Reserve Bank for the aforesaid class of transactions as enumerated in Schedule II, are (1) Foreign Exchange Management (Transfer or Issue of any Foreign Security) (Amendments) Regulations, 2004, (2) Foreign Exchange Management (Investment in Firm or Proprietary Concern in India) Regulations, 2000, (3) Foreign Exchange Management (Acquisition and Transfer of Immovable Property in India) Regulations,

2000, (4) Foreign Exchange Management(Guarantees) Regulations, 2000, (5) Foreign Exchange Management (Export and Import of Currency) Regulations, 2000. (6) Foreign Exchange Management (Deposits) Regulations, 2000. Overseas investments by Resident Individuals/Corporates have been greatly liberalised.

4. Prohibition regarding capital account transactions

Regulation 4 of the aforesaid Regulations provides that unless otherwise provided in FEMA Rules or FEMA Regulations no person is permitted to undertake or sell or draw foreign exchange to or from an authorised person for any capital account transaction. It has been specifically provided that no person resident outside India is permitted to make investment in India, in any form, in any company or partnership firm or proprietary concern or any entity, whether incorporated or not, which is engaged or proposes to engage in the following five types of businesses, namely—

(i)   in the business of chit fund, or
(ii) as Nidhi Company, or
(iii) in agricultural or plantation activities, or
(iv) in real estate business, or construction of farm houses, or
(v)   in trading in Transferable Development Rights (TDRs).

For the purposes of Regulation 4, "real estate business" would not include development of townships, construction of residential/commercial premises, roads or bridges. Thus, in respect of this real estate business in the form of construction or road, bridges, residential premises, etc. a person resident outside India could draw foreign exchange from an authorised person.

5. Method of payment for investment and declaration

Regulation 5 provides that the payment for investment would be made by remittance from abroad through normal banking channels or by debit to an account of the investor maintained with an authorised person in India in accordance with the regulations made by the Reserve Bank under FEMA. It is further provided by Regulation 6 that every person selling or drawing foreign exchange to or from an authorised person for a capital account transaction would be required to furnish to the Reserve Bank, a declaration in the form and within the time specified in the regulations relevant to the transaction.

6. Remittance of assets held by NRIs

Reference should be made to the A.P. (DIR Series) RBI Circular No. 62, dated January 31, 2004. The main aspects of the latest policy are analysed below:

(A) Eligibility for facility for remittance of assets:

The repatriation facility is available to the following category of persons:

(I) Foreign national (other than a citizen of Nepal or Bhutan or a Person of Indian Origin (PIO)] who:

(i)   has retired from an employment in India or

(ii) has inherited the assets from a person who was a resident in India or

(iii) a widow resident outside India and has inherited assets of her deceased husband who was an Indian Citizen, resident in India.

(II) NRI/PIO who acquired the assets in question, out of rupee resources when he was in India or by way of legacy/inheritance from a person who was a resident in India.

(B) Funds/assets eligible for repatriation:

(a) sale proceeds of immovable property,

(b) assets acquired by way of inheritance/legacy,

(c) a deposit with a bank or a firm or a company,

(d) provident fund balance or superannuation benefits,

(e) amount of claim or maturity proceeds of insurance policy,

(f) sale proceeds of shares, securities,

(g) any other asset held in India, in accordance with the provisions of the Act or Rules or Regulations made thereunder (as defined at Regulations 2(v) of Notification No. FEMA 13/2000-RB dated May 3, 2000).

(C) Purpose for which remittance is permissible:

The liberalised remitance facility is available for any bona fide purpose.

(D) General conditions to be satisfied for repatriation of assets:

(i) Documentary evidence in support of the acquisition of the funds/assets proposed to be remitted.

(ii) Undertaking and Certification relating to tax compliance.

(E) Specific conditions relating to repatriation of sale proceeds of immovable property:

(i) Repatriation of sale proceeds of immovable property, acquired out of Rupee funds is available subject to the condition that the property should have been held for a minimum period of 10 years. If such a property acquired out of Rupee funds is sold after being held for less than 10 years, remittance can be made, if the sale proceeds have been held by the NRI/PIO for the balance period in NRO Account (Savings/Term Deposits) or in any other eligible security, provided such investment is traced to the sale proceeds of the immovable property.

(ii) There is no lock-in-period in respect of immovable property acquired by way of—

  (a) Inheritance/legacy.

  (b) Foreign currency funds (through inward remittance or by debit to FCNR/NRE accounts

(F) Remittance procedure

(i) In case, the remittance is to be made in more than one instalment, the remittances of all instalments should be remitted through the same authorised dealer.

(ii) It is also clarified that the remittance facility is available even if the NRI/PIO/Foreign National is not maintaining any NRO account. However, the remittance should be routed through banking channel only, subject to tax compliance.

CHAPTER 15

Investment in shares, securities, units and other activities, etc. by an NRI in India

1. Introduction

The Reserve Bank of India notified Foreign Exchange Management (Transfer or Issue of Security by a Person Resident Outside India) Regulations, 2000, vide Notification No.FEMA 20/2000-RB dated 3.5.2000. These Regulations came into force from 1.6.2000. These Regulations seek to regulate investment in India by persons resident outside India, i.e. issue of any security by an Indian entity to a person resident outside India and purchase, sale of Indian securities by a person resident outside India. Thus, the Regulations regarding the purchase of shares, securities, units as also investment under Foreign Direct Investment Scheme, etc. are all contained in these Regulations. These have been amended on 3.10.2003.

2. Salient features of regulations

The salient features of Foreign Exchange Management (Transfer or Issue of Security by a person resident outside India) Regulations, 2000, are given below:

(1) These regulations seek to regulate investment in India by persons resident outside India, i.e. issue of any security by an Indian entity to a person resident outside India and purchase, sale of Indian securities by a person resident outside India.

(2) For the purpose of these Regulations the investment in India by person resident outside India has been divided in five categories and the regulations applicable have been specified in respective schedules, as under:

Schedule 1 — Foreign Direct Investment Scheme

Schedule 2	—	Investment by Foreign Institutional Investors under Portfolio Investment Scheme
Schedule 3	—	Investment by NRIs/OCBs under Portfolio Investment Scheme
Schedule 4	—	Purchase and sale of shares by NRIs/OCBs on non-repatriation basis
Schedule 5	—	Purchase and sale of securities other than shares or convertible debentures of an Indian company by persons resident outside India.
Schedule 6	—	Investment in an Indian V.C. by foreign V.C. Investor

(3) Citizens of Bangladesh, Pakistan or Sri Lanka resident outside India and entities in Bangladesh or Pakistan are not permitted to purchase shares or debentures issued by Indian companies or any other Indian security without the prior approval of Reserve Bank, in terms of Regulation No.5.

(4) General permission has been granted in Regulation No. 6 to any person resident outside India to purchase shares/convertible debentures offered on right basis by an Indian company which satisfies the conditions stipulated in sub-regulation (2) of the said Regulation. The right shares so acquired shall be subject to same condition regarding repatriability as are applicable to original shares.

(5) General permission has been granted to the transferee company or a new company consequent on merger or de-merger or amalgamation of Indian companies subject to the conditions specified in Regulation No. 7.

(6) An Indian company has been permitted to issue shares to its employees or employees of its joint venture/subsidiary abroad, who are resident outside India either directly to such employees or through a trust subject to the provision of Regulation No. 8.

(7) General permission has been granted in terms of Regulation No. 9 for transfer of shares/convertible debentures by a person resident outside India as under:

(i) for transfer of shares/convertible debentures held by a person resident outside India other than NRI/OCB to any person resident outside India, provided that the transferee should have obtained permission of Central Government if he had any previous venture or tie-up in India through investment in any manner or a technical collaboration or trade mark agreement in the same field or allied field in which the Indian company whose shares are being transferred is engaged;

(ii) NRIs/OCBs are permitted to transfer shares or convertible debentures of Indian company to another NRI/OCB;

(iii) A person resident outside India is permitted to transfer shares/debentures of an Indian company to a resident by way of gift.

(8) (i) Transfer of any security by a person resident in India to a person resident outside India would require approval of Reserve Bank.

(ii) For transfer of existing shares/convertible debentures of an Indian company by a resident to a non-resident by way of sale, the transferor should obtain an approval of the Central Government and thereafter apply to Reserve Bank. In such cases the Reserve Bank may permit the transfer subject to such terms and conditions including the price at which sale may be made.

(iii) Any other transfer not covered by the above referred provisions or the provisions of the Schedules would require the prior approval of Reserve Bank for which the application should be made on Form TSI. For arriving at the sale price of the shares in such cases the procedure indicated in Regulation 10B.2 should be followed.

(9) Reserve Bank has granted general permission for remittance of net sale proceeds (net of applicable taxes) of a security sold by a person resident outside India provided —

(a) the security is held on repatriation basis;

(b) security is sold on recognised stock exchange or the Reserve Bank's permission for sale of security and remittance of sale proceeds has been obtained; and

(c) a NOC/Tax Clearance Certificate from Income-tax authorities or an undertaking/ declaration as per the provisions of paragraph 3B.10 of ECM has been produced.

(10) The various schemes available to persons resident outside India for investment in Indian securities contained in the schedules are explained below in different paras.

3. Foreign Direct Investment Scheme

There are various schemes available under these Regulations for NRIs for investment in Indian securities. These are contained in various Schedules. Schedule No. I contains the Regulations regarding Foreign Direct Investment Scheme. The salient features of the Foreign Direct Investment Scheme as per the RBI Circular No.11 dated 16.5.2000, are given below:

SCHEDULE I
Foreign Direct Investment Scheme

(i)   Reserve Bank's automatic route
An Indian company which is not engaged in the activity or manufacture of items listed in Annexure A to this Schedule is permitted to issue shares to a person resident outside India upto the extent specified in Annexure B, on repatriation basis, provided—

- (a) The issuer company does not require an industrial licence
- (b) The shares are not being issued for acquiring existing shares of another Indian company;
- (c) If the person resident outside India to whom the shares are being issued proposes to be a collaborator, he should have obtained Central Government's approval if he had any previous investment collaboration/tie up in India in the same or allied field in which the Indian company issuing shares is engaged.

(ii)   Subject to compliance with the provisions of paragraph (i) above an Indian company which proposes to undertake activities in Annexure 'B' is permitted to issue shares/convertible debentures to persons resident outside India out of fresh capital issued for financing expansion programme for carrying on such activities.

(iii)   A trading company is permitted to issue shares/convertible debentures to the extent of 51 per cent of its capital to persons resident outside India. The remittance of dividend in respect of such shares would be permissible only when the company secures registration as an Export/Trading/Star Trading House.

(iv)   A SSI Unit which is not engaged in activity or manufacture of items included in Annexure 'A' to this Schedule may issue shares to non-residents upto 24 per cent of its capital. Such a company is permitted to issue shares beyond 24 per cent subject to ceilings specified in Annexure 'B' if (a) it gives up SSI status and (b) it is not engaged or does not propose to engage in manufacturing of items reserved for SSI sector.

(v)   EOUs or units in Free Trade Zones or in Software/Electronic Hardware Technology Parks are permitted to issue shares to persons resident outside India beyond 24 per cent subject to compliance with ceilings indicated in Annexure 'B'.

(vi) Issue of shares by an Indian company to a person resident outside India which are not covered by the provisions of sub-paragraph (i) to (v) above would require approval of SIA or FIPB.

(vii) An Indian company is permitted to issue fresh shares to the depository abroad for the purpose of raising resources through ADR or GDR mechanism subject to the conditions specified in paragraph No.4, 4A & 4B of the Schedule.

(viii) The price of shares & ADRs/ GDRs to be issued by the Indian company to persons resident outside India should be in accordance with the provisions of paragraph No. 5 and 5A of the Schedule as amended w.e.f. 18-6-2003.

(ix) The remittance of dividend to the persons resident outside India by an Indian company which is engaged in any of the industries in the consumer sector specified in Annexure 'E' or any other activity to which dividend balancing requirement under the Industrial Policy notified by Government of India is applicable, would be subject to the provisions of paragraph No. 6 of the Schedule as amended w.e.f. 18-6-2003.

(x) The rate of dividend on preference shares issued by an Indian company to a person resident outside India should not exceed 300 basis points over State Bank of India's prime lending rate, in terms of paragraph No. 7 of the Schedule.

(xi) The consideration for issue of shares to persons resident outside India under this scheme should be received either by way of inward remittance through normal banking channels or out of funds held in NRE/FCNR accounts of NRI/OCB investor.

(xii) The Indian company issuing shares to non-residents under this scheme should submit to Reserve Bank, reports as specified in paragraph 9 of the schedule.

(xiii) Reserve Bank's permission is necessary for retention abroad of share subscription received by Indian company from non-residents.

(xiv) It may be noted that there are no separate schemes for NRIs/OCBs for direct investment in India on repatriation basis. NRIs/OCBs are now on par with any other foreign investor and they may invest in the shares/convertible debentures issued by an Indian company under the Foreign Direct Investment Scheme.

(xv) Annexures A,B,C and D have been substituted w.e.f. 18-6-2003.

For further relaxation, please refer to the RBI.

4. Investment by foreign institutional investors (FIIs) under Portfolio Investment Scheme

The earlier regulations and procedure for investment by FIIs under Portfolio Investment Scheme mostly remain unchanged, and they are duly incorporated in Schedule 2 to these Regulations. It has also been made clear in this Schedule that the Reserve Bank would also consider applications from a domestic asset management company or a portfolio manager registered with SEBI as FII for managing the sub-account to make investment under the Portfolio Investment Scheme on behalf of persons resident outside India who are foreign citizens and body corporate registered outside India₁ as indicated in paragraph 4 of Schedule 2. Such investment would be restricted to 5 per cent of the equity capital or 5 per cent of the paid up value of each series of convertible debentures within the overall ceiling of 24 per cent or 40 per cent as applicable for FIIs for the purpose of Portfolio Investment Scheme. From 1-1-2004 on registered FII has to maintain an account regarding purchase and sale of shares/convertible debentures.

5. Portfolio Investment Scheme for NRIs on repatriation/non-repatriation basis

Schedule 3 of these Regulations is of great practical utility to most of NRIs. There is no change in the earlier scheme for portfolio investment by NRIs on repatriation/non-repatriation basis except that the requirement of grant of approval by designated branch of an authorised dealer valid for a period of 5 years at a time has been dispensed with under the new Regulations as amended w.e.f. 3-10-2003.

6. Purchase/sale of shares and convertible debentures by NRIs on non-repatriation basis

Schedule 4 to these Regulations contains various Rules regarding the purchase/sale of shares and convertible debentures by NRIs on non-repatriation basis. It may be noted here that there is no change in the earlier procedures/regulations for purchase and sale of shares/convertible debentures by NRIs on non-repatriation basis.

7. Purchase and sale of other securities

Schedule 5 to these regulations contains rules regarding the purchase and sale of securities other than shares/debentures by a on-resident. There are no changes in the regulations or procedure applicable for purchase and sale of other securities by NRIs on repatriation/non-repatriation basis and by FIIs on repatriation basis.

Scheduled 6, inserted w.e.f. 27-10-2003 is about investment in an Indian venture capital undertaking by a registered foreign venture capital investor.

8. Long-term capital gains on shares: Exemption under Section 10 (36)

The Finance Act, 2003 provides that any long-term capital gain regarding eligible equity shares in a company and purchased on or after 1-3-2003 but before 1-3-2004 would be exempt from tax. Eligible equity share means (i) any equity share in a company being a constituent of BSE-500 Index of the Stock Exchange, Mumbai as on 1-3-2003 and such transaction of purchase and sale are entered into on a recognised stock exchange in India; and (ii) any equity share in a company allotted through a public issue on or after 1-3-2003 and listed in a recognised stock exchange in India before 1-3-2004 and such transaction is entered into on a recognised stock exchange in India.

9. Other regulations

The Foreign Exchange Management (Transfer or issue of Security by a Person Resident Outside India) Regulations, 2000 contains other matters like acquisition of right shares for which detailed provisions have been made in Regulation 6. Regulation 7 contains various matters regarding the issue and acquisition of shares after merger or de-merger or amalgamation of Indian companies. The Employees Stock Options Scheme is becoming popular now-a-days. Hence, Regulation 8 of these Regulations contains detailed rules regarding the issue of shares under the Employees' Stock Options Scheme to persons resident outside India. As regards transfer of shares and convertible debentures of an Indian company by an NRI, detailed regulations are contained in Regulation No. 9. It has also been made clear that prior permission of the Reserve Bank is required in certain cases for transfer of securities by gift or sale, etc. as contained in Regulation No. 10. Regulation No. 11 of these Regulations makes it clear that no remittance of sale proceeds of an Indian security held by a person resident outside India would be made otherwise than in accordance with these Regulations and the conditions specified in the relevant Schedule. Hence, a reference to Schedules as discussed above becomes necessary for an NRI interested in the remittance of sale proceeds for which normally there is no problem in India. [For latest relaxations a reference to the Reserve Bank of India should be made].

CHAPTER 16

Deposits in India by an NRI

1. Introduction

This is another important chapter of great practical significance for the NRIs. Most of the NRIs are conversant with NRE and FCNR deposits in India. Likewise, deposits in NRO account and NRSR account are also well known. Under the FEMA, detailed Regulations have now been notified by the Reserve Bank of India known as "Foreign Exchange Management (Deposit) Regulations, 2000" vide RBI Notification No. FEMA 5/2000-RB dated 3.5.2000. These regulations have also been come into force from 1.6.2000. They have been amended w.e.f. 3-10-2003 when the general permission to OCBs was withdrawn. The detailed provisions regarding different types of accounts like FCNR(B) account, NRE account, NRO account, NRNR account, NRSR account, etc. are explained in the following paragraphs. Regulation No.4 of these Regulations contains permission for opening rupee/foreign currency deposits accounts by certain persons, namely, rupee/foreign currency accounts by foreign diplomatic missions and diplomatic personnel or their family members with an authorised dealer, subject to conditions contained in the Regulations and (b) Deposits with an authorised dealer in rupees by a person resident in Nepal and Bhutan, and (c) Deposits with authorised dealers by the U.N.O. and its subsidiary/affiliate bodies in India, or its officials in India. Regulation No.5 provides rules for deposit accounts opened with an authorised dealer by an NRI under various schemes, like the Non-resident (External) Account Scheme, which is explained in detail in topic 2 below and the FCNR(B) Scheme discussed in topic 3 below. Likewise, details regarding other types of accounts are given in different topics of this chapter.

2. Non-resident (External) Account Scheme

Regulation No.5 provides for deposit accounts opened with authorised dealers by an NRI under various schemes. These schemes have been detailed in various Schedules to these Regulations. Thus, Schedule 1 contains the details regarding the Non-resident (External) Account Scheme. The terms and conditions subject to which NRE accounts of NRIs can be maintained by authorised dealers or authorised banks have been specified in this Schedule. Generally, there is no change in the earlier NRE Account Scheme contained in Part B of Chapter 13 of ECM of RBI except that the limit for permitting overdraft in the account has been raised from Rs. 20,000 to Rs. 50,000. For the purpose of reporting to Reserve Bank authorised dealers/banks may follow the instructions contained in paragraph 13B.25 of ECM (Exchange Control Manual).

As per the Finance Act, 2005 interest on monies standing to the credit of an individual in a Non-Resident (External Account) would continue to be exempt even after 31.03.2005. Likewise, the interest payable by a scheduled bank to a Non-resident or to a person who is not ordinarily resident on deposits in foreign currency as approved by the Reserve Bank of India would continue to be exempt on or after 1.4.2005.

3. NRE account to RFC account

When the residential status of the account holder is changed from an NRI to a resident person, then para No. 7 of Schedule 1 provides that NRE accounts should be designated as resident accounts or the funds held in these accounts may be transferred to the RFC accounts (if the account holder is eligible for maintaining RFC account) at the option of the account holder immediately upon the return of the account holder to India for taking up employment or carrying on business or vocation or for any other purpose indicating intention to stay in India for an uncertain period. Where the account holder is only on a short visit to India, the account may continue to be treated as NRE account even during his stay in India. For detailed provisions regarding RFC account by a returning NRI, reference may be made to Chapter 17 of this book.

4. Foreign Currency (Non-Resident) Account (Banks) Scheme, i.e. FCNR (B)

The terms and conditions subject to which authorised dealers may open and maintain foreign currency accounts of NRIs under FCNR(B) schemes are specified in Schedule 2 to these Regulations as amended w.e.f. 3-10-2003. Generally, there is no change in the existing Part (B) scheme contained in Part B of Chapter 14 of ECM. As regards submission of data of inflows or outflows and outstanding deposits under the Scheme, the authorised dealers have to follow the procedure contained in paragraph 14B.10 of ECM, that is the Exchange Control Manual as advised by the RBI vide its Circular No.11 of 16.5.2000.

5. Non-Resident Ordinary Rupee(NRO) Account Scheme

The terms and conditions subject to which authorised dealers may open and maintain NRO accounts have been specified in Schedule 3 to these Regulations. These are similar to those contained in Part A—Section I of Chapter 13 of ECM, except that the ceiling on permitting overdraft in such accounts has been dispensed with. The authorised dealers may permit overdraft in such accounts as per their discretion and commercial judgement. For the rate of interest, inquiry from the bank concerned should be made.

6. Non-Resident (Non-Repatriable) Rupee (NRNR) Deposit Scheme

The terms and conditions subject to which NRNR account can be opened by authorised dealers in the name of any non-resident are specified in Schedule 4 which are similar to those contained in Part C of Chapter 13 of ECM. Such accounts can be opened by any non-resident in India.

7. Non-Resident (Special) Rupee (NRSR) Account Scheme

The terms and conditions subject to which authorised dealers can open and maintain NRSR account in the name of any NRI/PIO are specified in Schedule 5 to these Regulations. These are same as contained in Part

A—Section II of Chapter 13 of ECM. In terms of the provisions of Schedule 5, NRSR accounts will also be allowed to be opened and maintained by banks authorised to maintain accounts of non-residents, subject to the provisions of this Schedule.

8. Acceptance of deposit by a company in India from NRIs on repatriation basis

A company incorporated in India including NBFC registered with Reserve Bank has been granted general permission to accept deposits from NRIs on repatriation basis subject to terms and conditions specified in Schedule 6 to these regulations. General permission has also been granted for repayment of deposits by the company which has accepted deposits under the Scheme by inward remittance or by credit to NRE/FCNR account maintained with an authorised dealer of the bank in India subject to the conditions specified in paragraph (x) of this Schedule.

9. Acceptance of deposits by Indian proprietorship concern/firm or a company from NRIs on non-repatriation basis

General permission has been granted to Indian proprietorship concern[1] firm or a company (including Non-Banking Finance Company) registered with Reserve Bank to accept deposits from NRIs on non-repatriation basis subject to the terms and conditions specified in Schedule 7. The terms and conditions are similar to those stipulated in paragraph 10C.10(i) of ECM and erstwhile Notification No.FERA 196/99-RB dated 30th March, 1999.

Various other Rules and Regulations, for example, regarding acceptance of deposits from NRIs by issue of a commercial paper, etc. have been given in Regulation No.8 and Regulation No.9. It has also been made clear that any deposit between a person resident in India and a person outside India which is not covered by the provisions of FEMA or the aforesaid Regulations would require approval of the Reserve Bank.

10. Full convertibility of deposit scheme — Non-Resident Indians

With a view to providing full convertibility of deposit schemes for non-resident Indians and rationalizing the existing non-resident deposit schemes, RBI vide its circular No. 28 AP (DIR Series) dated 4 March 2002 had decided to discontinue NRNR Account and NRSR Account schemes with effect from 1 April 2002. Accordingly, with effect from 1 April 2002:

(a) Authorised dealers/authorized banks shall not accept any fresh deposits or open any fresh account, by way of renewal or otherwise, under the above two schemes.

(b) The existing accounts under NRNR account scheme may be continued only upto the date of maturity. The maturity proceeds of the deposits under NRNR Account Scheme shall be credited to the account-holder's Non-Resident (External) Rupee Account (NRE account), after giving notice to the account-holder that the maturity proceeds shall be credited to his NRE accounts. The account-holders may choose to credit the maturity proceeds to his NRE saving bank account or current account or open a fresh NRE term deposit account. The authorized dealers or authorized banks may also permit the account-holder, on his request to credit the maturity proceeds to NRO account. In case no reply is received from the account-holder, the maturity proceeds of deposits under NRNR account Scheme may be credited to his NRE account.

(c) The existing term deposits under the NRSR account scheme may be continued till the maturity and the maturity proceeds shall be credited to the Non-Resident (Ordinary) Rupee Account (NRO account) of the account-holder.

(d) The existing NRSR account, other than term deposit, shall not be continued after 30 September 2002, and may, at the option of the account-holder, be closed or balance thereof be credited to his NRO account on or before that date. For this purpose, a notice to the account-holders may be given and in case no reply is received, the said NRSR account may be closed and the balance transferred to the NRO account of the account-holder.

While the facilities currently available to the account-holders for premature withdrawal continue, in the event of premature closure of the term deposits, under both the schemes, the option of reinvesting the proceeds will, however, be restricted to the NRO account of the account-holder.

11. NRNR, NRSR Accounts to be discontinued on maturity

The Reserve Bank of India (RBI) had decided to discontinue rupee schemes of non-Resident Non-Repatriable account (NRNR) and Non-Resident (Special) account (NRSR) with effect from 1 April 2002 in extension of its earlier circular to bring these schemes under full convertibility.

RBI had issued a notification on 4 March 2002, allowing full convertibility of deposit schemes of NRIs like NRNR and NRSR accounts with effect from 1 April 2002. Accordingly, banks were asked not to accept fresh deposits or open any fresh account, by way of renewal or otherwise, under these two schemes. The decision to discontinue was intended to rationalise the existing non-resident deposit schemes, RBI said in the notification. The existing accounts under NRNR and NRSR would be allowed to continue only up to the date of maturity. However, other than term-deposits under NRSR account should not be continued after 30 September 2002.

The maturity proceeds of the deposits under NRNR should be credited to the account-holder's Non-Resident (External) account (NRE), after giving notice to the account-holder, RBI told banks. Thus, the existing term deposits will carry interest at the contracted rate till date of maturity.

However, the account-holder may choose to credit the maturity proceeds to his NRE savings account or current account or open a fresh NRE term deposit account, and banks can also permit the account-holder to credit them to Non-Resident (Ordinary) account (NRO).

NRNR account-holders have the option to directly credit maturity proceeds to NRE account, but not to Foreign Currency (Non-Resident) Accounts (Banks) scheme (FCNR-B).

The proceeds of NRNR deposits can be credited to NRE account only on maturity, and, in case of premature withdrawal, they should be credited only to NRO account.

For the latest relaxations, please make a reference to the Reserve Bank of India.

CHAPTER 17

RFC account of a returning NRI and investment abroad

1. Introduction

An NRI returning to India permanently at some time and becoming a resident in India is interested in knowing the types of Foreign Currency Accounts which he can maintain in India. Similarly, he will also be interested in knowing Regulations regarding direct investment in foreign currency securities other than by way of direct investment. The first types of Regulations are contained in Foreign Exchange Management (Foreign Currency Accounts by a person Resident in India) Regulations, 2000. The other set of Regulations regarding an investment by a returning NRI in India becoming a resident or any other resident person abroad are contained in Foreign Exchange Management (Transfer or Issue of any Foreign Security) Regulations, 2000. Both these Regulations came into force from 1.6.2000. The salient features of both these Regulations are analysed in this chapter.

2. Opening, holding and maintaining a resident foreign currency (RFC) account

A person resident in India as per Regulation No. 5 of Foreign Exchange Management (Foreign Currency Accounts by a Person Resident in India) Regulations, 2000, may open, hold, and maintain with an authorised dealer in India, a Foreign Currency Account, to be known as a Resident Foreign Currency (RFC) Account, out of foreign exchange—

(a) received as pension or any other superannuation or other monetary benefits from his employer outside India; or

(b) realised on conversion of the assets referred to in Section 6(4) of FEMA, and repatriated to India; or

(c) received or acquired as gift or inheritance from person resident outside India as referred in Section 6(4) of FEMA; or

(d) acquired as gift or inheritance from a person referred to in Section 9(c) of FEMA.

(e) received as proceeds of life insurance policy claims, etc. in foreign currency (w.e.f. 1-1-2004).

The funds in a RFC Account opened or held or maintained would be free from all restrictions regarding utilisation of foreign currency balances including any restriction on investment in any form, by whatever name, called, outside India. In some cases, a foreign currency account is also allowed to be maintained outside India by LIC or a shipping or airline company, etc.

RFC Scheme came into force with effect from 7.9.1992. Citizens of India or persons of Indian origin who having been residents outside for a continuous period of less than one year and who become persons residents in India or on or after 18th April, 1992 are eligible for opening RFC accounts. Persons holding RIFEE permits or re-conversion facility opting to open the RFC account are also eligible. The eligible assets which can be credited to the RFC account are foreign exchange assets acquired or held otherwise than in contravention of the FERA and FEMA by an eligible person, while he was the resident outside India (Non-resident) in the form of deposits in banks outside India, investments in foreign currency shares or securities or immovable properties situated outside India or investments in business, etc. outside India and include foreign exchange earnings through employment, through business or vocation, outside India taken up or commenced by such person while he was resident outside India. Any eligible person can open the RFC account with an authorised dealer. The application for this purpose has to be made in Form RFC and must be accompanied with the following documents:

(a) An attested copy of relevant pages of passport, giving the passport particulars, date of arrival in India and particulars of residence outside India;

(b) Documentary evidence to show the funds proposed to be credited to the account are eligible for the purpose, The RFC account can be opened in any permitted foreign currency.

All types of accounts, namely, current, saving, and fixed deposits, in joint accounts can be opened under this scheme. The rate of interest on the deposits under the scheme is left to the discretion of the authorised dealer. Normally, no loan or overdraft would be allowed either directly or indirectly against balances in RFC account.

3. Tax heaven for returning Indians via RFC account

Resident Foreign Currency A/c is the best solution for all those NRIs who are now permanently coming back to India. The FCNR A/c as also NRE A/c of the Non-Resident Indian while coming back to India permanently should be immediately converted into Resident Foreign Currency A/c (RFC) to achieve the best investment planning.

As per para 5A a resident individual may open, hold and maintain a Resident Foreign Currency (Domestic) A/c regarding certain receipts and shall not bear any interest.

4. EEFC Account

It is provided by Regulation No. 4 of Foreign Exchange Management (Foreign Currency Account by a Person Resident in India) Regulations. 2000, that a person resident in India may open, hold and maintain with an authorised agent in India, a Foreign Currency Account to be known as Exchange Earner's Foreign Currency (EEFC) Account, subject to the terms and conditions of this Scheme specified in the Schedule.

Thus, the earners of foreign exchange are allowed to retain upto 25% of the inward remittance in foreign currency in such EEFC accounts. However, in the case of hundred percent export-oriented units and units in export processing zones, software technology parks or electronic hardware technology parks, upto 100 per cent of foreign exchange is allowed to be credited to the EEFC accounts. Any other person resident in India is allowed to credit 50% to EEFC A/c out of the foreign exchange earnings. The exporters who are allowed by the RBI to open foreign currency account abroad, are not allowed to open EEFC accounts. Thus, the NRIs returning to India in particular and the other residents in India in general who are exporters, should remember the provisions regarding the EEFC and take advantage of the same. The interest earned by a resident on EEFC account balances is, however, not exempt from income tax.

5. Direct investment outside India by a returning NRI or a resident in India

Under the Foreign Exchange Management (Transfer or Issue of any Foreign Security) Regulations, 2000 notified by Reserve Bank of India vide Notification No.FEMA 19/2000-RB dated 3.5.2000, various Regulations have been made to regulate acquisition and transfer of a foreign security by a person resident in India. These have been amended from time. Thus, an NRI returning to India and becoming a resident in India in particular should know the regulations regarding investment in Overseas Joint Ventures and Wholly Owned Subsidiaries as also investment in shares and securities issued outside India. As mentioned in Chapter l6, topic 3 an NRE account has to be converted to RFC account by a returning NRI. Hence, this account plays an important role in addition what is mentioned in RFC account above. It has also been mentioned in Regulation No.4 about the general permission being granted to the residents including the returning NRIs, for purchase/acquisition of securities out of funds held in RFC accounts; issued as bonus shares on existing holding of foreign currency shares and sale of shares/securities so acquired. Likewise, general permission has been granted to a person resident in India for purchase of securities out of their foreign currency resources outside India as also for sale of securities so acquired. For this purpose, the Regulations have been divided into two parts, namely Part I dealing with direct investment outside India and Part II dealing with investment in foreign securities other than by way of direct investment. Part 1 of these Regulations contains various limits for direct investment abroad. Part II contains various regulations regarding investment in foreign securities other than by way of direct investment upto various limits as given in said regulations in detail. It has also been laid down in the regulations in Part 2 that the Reserve Bank would consider application from residents for acquisition of foreign securities in various cases like acquisition of qualification shares for becoming a director of a company outside India, purchase of foreign securities under

ADRs/GDRs Stock Option Scheme, by resident employees of Indian Software Companies including working directors provided purchase consideration does not exceed US Dollars 50,000 or its equivalent in a block of five calendar years. The Reserve Bank vide its Circular No.3 (A.P DIR Series) dated 22nd June, 2000 issued guidelines regarding Indian Direct Investment by Joint Ventures JV/Wholly owned Subsidiaries (WOS) outside India. Reference may also be made to A.P. (Dir series)(2002-2003) Circular No. 107 dated 19-6-2003. For the latest provisions and relaxations, please refer to the latest RBI Regulations.

CHAPTER 18

Miscellaneous regulations under FEMA and NRIs

1. Introduction

The most important provisions of FEMA and the various Regulations notified under FEMA of practical use by the NRIs have been described in detail in Chapters 11 to 17. There are other miscellaneous Regulations concerning the different subjects like acquisition and transfer of immovable properties outside India, investment in a firm or proprietary concern in India, borrowing or lending in foreign exchange or rupees. establishment of a branch or place of business in India by an NRI, special provisions for Nepal and Bhutan, export of goods and services, possession and retention of foreign currency, guarantees, insurance, remittance of assets, foreign contributions, outbound investments, etc. are discussed in this chapter. The relevant Regulation governing a particular provision has also been described by its proper name at the relevant place. For latest changes therein reference should be made to he RBI.

2. Acquisition and transfer of immovable property outside India

The Reserve Bank notified the Foreign Exchange Management (Acquisition and Transfer of Immovable Property outside India) Regulations, 2000 vide Notification No. FEMA 7/2000-RB dated 3.5.2000. These regulations are effective from 1.6.2000. In terms of these regulations, acquisition or transfer of any immovable property outside India by a person resident in India would require prior approval of Reserve Bank except in the following cases:

(i)   Property held outside India by a foreign citizen resident in India;

(ii) Property acquired by a person on or before 8th July, 1947 and held with the permission of Reserve Bank;
(iii) Property acquired by way of gift or inheritance from persons referred to in (ii) above;
(iv) Property purchased out of funds held in RFC account.

General permission has also been granted to a person resident in India for transfer of a property acquired by him in terms of sub-paragraphs (iii) & (iv) above to his relative as specified in the Explanation to Regulation No.5, who is also a person resident in India. From 13-10-2003 as per Regulation 5(3) the RBI may permit an Indian company to acquire immovable property out of India.

3. Investment in firm or proprietary concern in India

Another important Regulation notified by the Reserve Bank of India was Foreign Exchange Management (Investment in Firm or Proprietary Concern in India) Regulations, 2000 notified by the Reserve Bank vide Notification No.FEMA 24/2000-RB dated 3rd May, 2000. These regulations are also in force from 1.6.2000. These were amended on 2001-2002. These regulations provide that except as otherwise provided in the Act or rules or regulations made or directions or orders issued thereunder, any investment by way of contribution to the capital of a firm or a proprietary concern or association of persons in India by a person resident outside India requires prior approval of Reserve Bank. In terms of Regulation No.4, Reserve Bank has granted general permission to an Indian citizen or a PIO [as defined in Regulation 2(vi)] resident outside India to make investment by way of contribution to the capital of a firm or a proprietary concern in India not engaged in print media on non-repatriation basis subject to conditions mentioned therein. In terms of Regulation No.5, general permission has also been granted to a firm or proprietary concern to make payment in rupees to or for credit of the non-resident Indian or a person of Indian origin the amount invested in the said firm/concern and income accruing on such investment by way of profit of such person. There is no change in the existing regulations governing such investment by NRIs/PIOs in a firm/proprietary concern on non-repatriation basis.

4. Borrowing or lending in foreign exchange

The RBI framed the Foreign Exchange Management (Borrowing or Lending in Foreign Exchange) Regulations, 2000 vide Notification No.FEMA 3/2000-RB, dated 3rd May, 2000. In terms of these regulations, approval of Reserve Bank would be necessary for any borrowing or lending in foreign exchange by any person resident in India except those covered in Regulation Nos. 4 and 5. The existing schemes namely the US $ 5 million scheme, US $ 10 million scheme (of paragraph 7B.8A of ECM) and scheme for raising of foreign currency loans by residents from Non-resident Indians not exceeding US $ 2,50,000 (explained in the Schedule) would continue to be operated by Reserve Bank. Any foreign currency borrowing which is not covered by these schemes or by the provisions of Regulation Nos. 4 and 5 would require approval of Government of India as well as Reserve Bank of India. Any lending by a person resident in India to a person resident outside India which is not covered by Regulation Nos.4 and 5 of these regulations would also be subject to Reserve Banks approval. These have been modified by the RBI from time to time, e.g. Circular No. 10, dt. 5.9.2000, No. 23 dt. 17.9.2002, No. 36 dt. 14.11.2003, No. 5 dt. 1.8.2005 and Master Circular dt. 1.7.2005, etc.

5. Borrowing or lending in rupees

The Reserve Bank of India notified the Foreign Exchange Management (Borrowing and Lending in Rupees) Regulations, 2000 vide Notification No.FEMA 4/2000-RB, dated 3rd May, 2000. These have been amended from time to time. The salient features of these regulations are given below:

(i) These regulations relate to borrowing and lending in rupees by a person resident in India from/to a person resident outside India.

(ii) Regulation No.4 provides for permission for borrowings in rupees by a person resident in India on non-repatriation basis from NRIs subject to the conditions referred to therein. This corresponds to general permission granted vide erstwhile Notification No.FERA 200/99-RB. dated 30th March, 1999 (of paragraph 10D.8 of ECM).

(iii) Regulation No. 5 provides for general permission for borrowings by an Indian company from NRIs/OCBs on non-repatriation/repatriation basis subject to terms and conditions specified therein by issue of non-convertible debentures. These provisions correspond to the provisions of erstwhile Notification No.FERA 213/99-RB, dated 1st November, 1999 (of paragraph 10C.7(ii) and 10C.15 of the ECM).

(iv) Regulation No. 6 provides for restrictions on use of borrowed fund.

(v) Regulation No. 7 provides for general permission to authorised dealers to grant rupee loans to NRIs against security of shares or immovable property in India subject to the conditions specified therein (corresponding to the provision of paragraph 10D.2(i) of the ECM).

(vi) Regulation No. 8 provides for grant of rupee loans by authorised dealer or housing finance institutions approved by National Housing Bank in NRIs for acquisition of residential accommodations subject to the terms and conditions referred to therein (corresponding to paragraph 10D.2(ii) and (iii) of the ECM).

(vii) Regulation No. 11 provides for permitting an overdraft by an authorised dealer in rupee accounts of its overseas branches/correspondents/head office not exceeding five hundred lakhs in aggregate. Authorised dealers may follow the instructions contained in the paragraph 5A.10 of the ECM in this regard.

(viii) Any borrowing or lending in rupees by a person resident in India from/to a person resident outside India which is not covered by the provisions of the Act or Rules or these Regulations would require approval of Reserve Bank.

6. Establishment of a branch or place of business in India

The Reserve Bank of India notified the Foreign Exchange Management (Establishment in India of a Branch or Office or other Place of Business) Regulations, 2000, vide Notification No. FEMA 22/2000-RB dated 3rd May, 2000. These have also come into force from 1.6.2000. These have been amended from time to time. In terms of these regulations establishment of a branch or liaison office of project office or any other place of business in India by any entity resident outside India other than a banking company requires approval of Reserve Bank. The application for permission should be made to Reserve Bank, Central Office in Form FNC I. A banking company registered or incorporated outside India has been permitted to open a branch or office in India if it has obtained necessary permission under the Banking Regulation Act, 1949. In terms of Regulation No. 4, persons who are citizen of Pakistan, Bangladesh, Sri Lanka, Afghanistan, Iran or China require approval of Reserve Bank for opening of a branch or office or a place of business in India. The list of permissible activities which can be undertaken by a branch or a liaison office have been specified in the schedules. A project or site office has been permitted to undertake activities relating and incidental in execution of project in India. Authorised dealers have been permitted to allow remittance of profit by a branch and remittance of surplus after completion of the project by the project office subject to terms and conditions specified in Regulation No. 7.

Along with the above regulations, another regulation, namely, Foreign Exchange Management (Issue of Security in India by a Branch Office or Agency of a Person Resident Outside India) Regulations, 2000 notified vide Notification No.FEMA 2/2000-RB dated 3rd May, 2000 should also be remembered. In terms of the these regulations, amended from time to time, any transfer or issue of any security or a foreign security in India by a branch, office or agency in India of any person resident outside India which is not covered by the provisions of the FEMA Rules or FEMA Regulations would require prior approval of the Reserve Bank.

7. Special provisions for Nepal and Bhutan

Under the provisions of Section 3 of FEMA there are restrictions on dealing in foreign exchange. However, these restrictions have been relaxed by the RBI in so far as transactions with Nepal and Bhutan are concerned, vide Notification No.FEMA 17/2000-RB, dated 3rd May, 2000. Vide this Notification, the Reserve Bank has directed that the prohibitions imposed by clauses (b), (c) and (d) of Section 3 relating to making payment to or for credit of any person resident outside India, or receiving otherwise through an authorised person any payment by order or on behalf of a person resident outside India, or entry into any financial transactions in India as consideration for or in association with acquisition or creation or transfer of a right to acquire any asset outside India would not be applicable for any transaction entered into in Indian rupees by or with (a) citizen of India, Nepal or Bhutan, resident in Nepal or Bhutan, (b) a branch in Nepal or Bhutan of a company or corporation in India or Nepal or Bhutan or (c) a branch in Nepal or

Bhutan of a partnership firm or otherwise of citizens of India, Nepal and Bhutan. These regulations have also come into effect on 1.6.2000.

8. Export of goods and services

The Reserve Bank of India notified the Foreign Exchange Management (Export of Goods and Services) Regulations, 2000, vide Notification No. FEMA 23/2000-RB dated 3rd May, 2000. These regulations have come into force from 1.6.2000. These have been amended from time to time.

9. Possession and retention of foreign currency

In terms of provisions of Section 9 of FEMA, the Reserve Bank notified the Foreign Exchange Management (Possession and Retention of Foreign Currency) Regulations, 2000 vide Notification No.FEMA 11/2000-RB dated 3.5.2000. These regulations have come into force from 1.6.2000. In terms of provisions of Section 9 of the FEMA, the Reserve Bank has specified the limit for possession and retention of foreign currency by a person resident in India, under these regulations. The salient features of these regulations are given below:

(a) Authorised persons have been permitted to possess foreign currency and coins in accordance with the limits, if any, advised to them by the Reserve Bank.

(b) There is no restriction on possession of foreign coins by any person.

(c) Any person resident in India is permitted to retain in aggregate foreign currency not exceeding US $ 2000 or its equivalent in the form of currency note/bank notes or travellers cheques acquired by him from sources referred to in clauses (a) to (d) of sub-regulation (iii) of Regulation No.3.

(d) A person resident in India but not permanently resident therein is permitted to possess foreign currency notes, bank notes and travellers cheques without limit if the foreign currency was acquired when he was resident outside India and was brought into India and declared to customs authorities where such declaration was required to be made.

10. Guarantees

The Reserve Bank of India notified the Foreign Exchange Management (Guarantees) Regulations, 2000 vide Notification No. FEMA 8/2000-RB, dated 3rd May, 2000.

11. Insurance

The Reserve Bank of India notified the Foreign Exchange Management (Insurance) Regulations. 2000 vide Notification No. FEMA 12/2000-RB, dated 3rd May, 2000. These have been amended from time to time. These have also come into force from 1.6.2000.

12. Remittance of assets

The Reserve Bank notified the Foreign Exchange Management (Remittance of Assets) Regulations, 2000, vide Notification No.FEMA 13/2000-RB, dated 3.5.2000. These regulations came into force from 1.6.2000. These have been amended later. Remittance of capital assets in India held by a person whether resident in or outside India would require approval of the Reserve Bank except to the extent provided in the FEMA or FEMA Rules or FEMA Regulations made under the Act. The salient aspects of the above regulations are given below:

(i) Under the existing provisions (paragraph 11D.5 of ECM) remittance of assets by foreign nationals not permanently resident in India, on their retirement from India were allowed by Reserve Bank in instalments. Similarly, foreign born widows of Indian nationals were also permitted by Reserve Bank to transfer their assets by remittance from India in instalment (of Paragraph 11D.6 of ECM).

(ii) In terms of Regulation No. 4, authorised dealers have been permitted to allow remittance of assets of a person referred to in sub-regulation (2) who has retired from India or who has inherited assets from a person who was a resident of India, or remittance of assets in India of a foreign born widow of an Indian national resident outside India in annual instalments of US $ 1 million subject to the terms and conditions mentioned therein.

(iii) Authorised dealers have been permitted to allow remittance of balance amount held in a bank account by a foreign student after completion of his studies.

(iv) General permission has also been granted to Indian entities to make remittance towards their share of contribution to provident fund or superannuation/pension fund in respect of their expatriate staff who are resident in India but not permanently resident therein.

(v) Remittance of winding up proceeds of a branch in India, remittance of legacy, bequest or inheritance or remittance of assets on hardship grounds would require approval of Reserve Bank as stated in Regulation No. 6. The Reserve Bank of India on 20-3-2002 decided to allow Non-resident Indians of Indian origin to remit upto 1,00,000 per year out of assets in India acquised by way of inheritance.

13. Foreign contributions

Though gifts by NRIs to their relatives and friends in India are permitted, yet gifts to political parties, etc. are not permitted in general. These are regulated by various regulations. Foreign contributions (Regulations) Act, 1976 regulate the acceptance and utilisation of foreign contribution or foreign hospitality by certain persons or associations, with a view to insuring that Parliamentary Institutions, Political Associations, and Academic and other voluntary organisations as well as individuals working in important areas of national life may function in a manner consistence with the values of a Sovereign Democratic Republic and for matters connected therewith or incidental thereto. Foreign Contribution (Regulations) Rules, 1976 laid down various regulations for governing the procedure in the matter of applications for obtaining prior permission to receive foreign contribution or foreign hospitality. For example. Rule 2 of these rules provides that an application for obtaining prior permission of the Central Government to receive foreign contribution has to be made in either Form FC-1 or FC-1A or Form FC-2. An application for registration of an association for acceptance of foreign contribution has to be made in FC-8. The intimation as to the receipt of foreign contribution by an association has to be given every year beginning on the first day of April in Form FC-3 in duplicate within 4 months of the closure of the year. Likewise, there are other rules governing different types of foreign contributions.

14. Outbound Investments

Very often an expression is used by NRIs for outbound investments. It is the investment abroad by a company incorporated in India. An individual resident in India, an Indian partnership firm or any other resident entity is not permitted to make investment abroad, except under the special Regulation made under FEMA. Indian corporates can make the investment on the basis of permission obtained from the Reserve Bank of India or the authorised dealer. The permissions for such investment are made as fast track route or otherwise. These should be read with the provisions governing EEFC account, etc. as discussed in Chapter 17 in detail. It would not be out of place to know the further liberalisation in the matter of overseas investment or outbound investment which has now been allowed for individual professionals. *The Financial Express,* New Delhi dated 29.1.2001 contained a news item to the effect that overseas investment has been thrown open to individuals as a further step towards capital account convertibility. Under the revised policy, on overseas investments by the RBI, individual professionals like chartered accountants or software consultants among others, would be the preferred category to be allowed for such proposals. However, such cases would be studied on a case-to-case basis by RBI to decide on the limit and granting of the final permission. As mentioned, overseas investments was only allowed for corporates in the past. Individuals were permitted in exceptional cases, where the person concerned had to be a non-resident Indian with a resident foreign currency account, i.e. RFC account to service such investments or invest under the employee stock option scheme. However, these routes continue to exist along with the new ones. As per the revised guidelines which will be notified in due course, the individuals can invest overseas from proceeds earned out of the existing EEFC account or fees/shares earned in foreign currency in lieu of services rendered to the foreign partners. They would also be able to purchase foreign currency from the domestic market and go ahead with the investment. NRIs returning to India as also resident professionals in particular should keep themselves in touch with the revised regulations and guidelines in regard to overseas investment and also other matters concerning foreign exchange. For latest relaxations please refer to the Reserve Bank of India.

CHAPTER 19

FAQs (frequently asked questions) of NRIs and answers

Residential Status

Q.1.   I left India about 22 years ago. I am settled in the U.S.A. I wish to come to India very often and still maintain my status as NRI for income tax purpose. How can I do that?

Ans.   See Chapter 1, topic 3.

Q.2.   I was not born in India. I was born in the U.K. However, my father was born in India. I visit India for about 40 to 50 days in a year. Can I be an NRI?

Ans.   Yes. See Chapter 1, topic 4.

Q.3.   I want to leave India for the first time on 8.7.2007 for employment in the U.S.A. I do not want to be a resident of India. I wish to enjoy the status of NRI for the financial year 2007-2008. What precautions should be taken by me so that I can become an NRI?

Ans.   See Chapter 1, topic 7.

Q.4.   I am an NRI settled in Dubai. Please let me know the precautions which I should take when I come to India on leave so that I am able to retain my NRI status?

Ans.   See Chapter 1, topic 8.

Q.5.   Is it possible that I may remain a resident but not ordinarily resident in India for some years even after my permanent return from the USA to India?

Ans.   Yes. See Chapter 1, topic 9.

Q.6.   I am the karta of a Hindu undivided family. I am an NRI for the last 15 years. Some of the members of my family are staying in

India permanently. Is it possible to have NRI status for my Hindu undivided family also?

Ans.   Yes. See Chapter 1, topic 10.

Tax Liability

Q.7.   What incomes in India will be liable to income tax when I am an NRI for the last 11 years?

Ans.   See Chapter 2, topic 3.

Q.8.   I am an NRI. I have sent some technical know-how to an Indian Company. I will be getting a royalty of about Rs. 12 lakh during the financial year 2007-2008. Will I be liable to income tax on Rs. 12 lakhs?

Ans.   Yes. See Chapter 2, topic 3.

Q.9.   During the financial year ending on 31.3.2007 my net income from house property in India by way of rent is Rs. 20 lakh. Will I be liable to income tax only or income tax surcharge also?

Ans.   You will also be liable to an income tax surcharge of 10 per cent as your total income exceeds Rs. 10,00,000. Education Cess of 2% would also be payable by you. Also see Chapter 2, topic 4 and 7.

Q.10.   I would be returning to India for permanent residence in India in the month of May 2007. Is it possible to plan my income so that I am not required to pay any income tax in India on my return?

Ans.   Yes. See Chapter 2, topic 9.

Income of Spouse and Children

Q.11   I made a gift of Rs. 5 lakh to my wife living in India. I am an NRI having some taxable income in India. Will the income of my wife out of gifted money be liable to income tax in her hands or in my hands?

Ans.   You will be liable to tax on the income of your wife out of gifts sent by you. See Chapter 3, topic 3.

Q.12.   I am an NRI. My minor child aged 15 years is studying in Mayo College, Ajmer. I have made a gift of Rs. 15 lakh in his name and he is having interest income therefrom. Will the minor son be liable to tax in his own name in respect of the interest income?

Ans.   No. The income of the minor will be added in your hands. Refer to Chapter 3, topic 4.

Q.13. I have a minor daughter aged 12 who is studying in a school in India. She is staying in a hostel. I have gifted Mutual Fund Units worth Rs. 20 lakh in her name. Will the dividend of mutual funds be liable to tax in my name?

Ans. No. This is because the dividend from mutual funds is completely exempt from tax under Section 10(35) of the I.T. Act. See also Chapter 3, topic 4.

Q.14. I propose to make a gift of Rs. 12 lakh to the wife of my eldest son, living in New Delhi. I am an NRI. My rental income in India is about Rs. 1 lakh per year. Is there any tax liability in respect of the aforesaid gift to my daughter-in-law?

Ans. Yes. The entire income of your daughter-in-law from the aforesaid gift will be added in your hands because of Section 64 of the I.T. Act. See Chapter 3, topic 5.

Q.15. My eldest son is studying in a business school at New Delhi. He is 21 years old. Out of gifts sent by me to him in the past his net rental income from house property is Rs. 5 lakh per annum. Will I be liable to income tax thereon?

Ans. No. your son will be liable to pay tax in his own name as a resident person. See Chapter 3, topic 6.

Q.16. I and my wife are NRIs. We are both working in the USA. Out of our earnings we have invested the money in India in the purchase of a residential flat which has been given on rent. The flat is in our joint names. Both of us have contributed money for investment in the said flat out of our funds in equal proportion. The net rental income of the flat during the financial year 2007-2008 is going to be Rs. 90,000. There is no other income in India either in my name or in the name of my wife.

Ans. As the house property is in joint names in equal share, the net income from house property will Rs. 45,000 for you and Rs. 45,000 for your wife. As this is below Rs. 1,10,000 exemption limit, none of you will be liable to tax in India. See Chapter 3, topic 9. Please do remember that the exemption limit for resident women tax payers is Rs. 1,45,000 for the A.Y 2008-2009.

Exempted Income

Q.17.   Interest income on deposits in Non-resident (External) Account would be Rs. 2,50,000 during the financial year 2007-2008. I am an NRI. Will I be liable to any tax in India?

Ans.   No. See Chapter 4, topic 2.

Q.18.   I am an NRI for the last six years. Before leaving India, I had made an investment in agricultural land in Ajmer. My annual income from agriculture is approximately Rs. 2 lakh. I have no other income in India. Am I liable to any income tax in India?

Ans.   No. See Chapter 4, topic 5(a).

Q.19.   During the month of April, 2007, I, as an NRI, was lucky in getting a prize of Rs. 5 lakh in Horse Racing in Mumbai and Calcutta. I feel that this income is not liable to tax as it is my casual income.

Ans.   No. You will be liable to income tax in respect of horse race winnings of Rs. 5 lakh.

Q.20.   My only income in India as an NRI is interest on deposits in NR (External) Account. I want to know whether this is exempt from income tax.

Ans.   Yes. It is exempt from income tax. See Chapter 4, topic 5(c).

Q.21.   As an NRI I have made investments in shares and units of UTI and Mutual Funds. My dividend income during the year ending on 31.3.2007 will be Rs. 6 lakh and dividend from Mutual Funds units was Rs. 8 lakh. What is my tax liability?

Ans.   You are not liable to income tax on the above income because of complete exemption under Section 10(34) & (35). See Chapter 4, topic 5(e).

Capital Gains

Q.22.   I am an NRI. On the sale of one house property, I have made a long-term capital gain of Rs. 6 lakh. However, I have lost Rs. 5,70,000 on the sale of long-term shares. I have no other income in India. Will I be liable to income tax in India on capital gains?

Ans.   No. The loss of Rs. 5,70,000 will be adjusted against the long-term capital gain of Rs. 6 lakh, The net long-term capital gain being Rs. 30,000 only and being below the exemption limit, you are not liable to any tax. Also see Chapter 5, topic 1.

Q.23.   I am an NRI. On the sale of certain silver utensils used by me on ceremonial occasions in India, I have made a gain of Rs. 1,20,000. I have no other income in India. Am I liable to any tax in India?

Ans.   No. You are not liable to any tax in India as the gain is in respect of personal effects, which are not treated as capital asset. See Chapter 5, topic 2.

Q.24.   I inherited property from my grandfather who remained its owner for 20 years, The inheritance took place in January, 2007. I wish to sell that property for Rs. 20 lakh, Will I be liable to any tax or can I get any exemption on the gain, if any.

Ans.   The period your grandfather held property would be considered as the period of holding the property by you. Thus, it will be a long-term capital asset. After the application of Cost Inflation Index, if there is any gain, you would be required to pay income-tax at 20 per cent on the long-term capital gain, if any. If you invest the net capital gain in the NHAI or REC Bonds then, you will be completely exempt from income tax under Section 54EC. See Chapter 5, topics 3 & 6.

Q.25.   I am an NRI. I have sold my self-occupied residential house property in New Delhi and have made a net long-term capital gain of Rs. 6 lakh. I wish to buy another property. What can I do to get complete exemption from income tax?

Ans.   You should invest the sum of Rs. 6 lakh being the long-term capital gain in the purchase of a house property in New Delhi, or any place in India, so as to get exemption. Also see Chapter 5, topic 4.

Q.26.   I own two residential houses. I am an NRI. I have sold a plot of land and made a long-term capital gain of Rs. 12 lakh. Can I buy a house property and get complete exemption from income tax?

Ans.   No, because you own more than one residential house property. See Chapter 5, topic 5.

Q.27.   I have made a long-term capital gain on the sale of debentures and shares of Rs. 15 lakh. The sale price of the shares, etc. is Rs. 32 lakh. I have no property in India. I wish to construct one house property in India and get exemption from tax on capital gains. Can I do so?

Ans.   Yes. You should invest the sum of Rs. 32 lakh in the construction of a residential house property within three years from the date of sale of the shares, etc. Also refer to Chapter 5, topic 5.

Q.28.   I am an NRI. I have sold one plot of land for Rs. 40 lakh and made a long-term capital gain of Rs. 16 lakh. I wish to buy one flat in New Delhi costing Rs. 30 lakh. What will be the amount of long-term capital gain liable to income tax in India?

Ans.   If you invest the entire sale proceeds of Rs. 40 lakh in the purchase of a house property in India, you will be exempt from tax. However, as only a sum of Rs. 30 lakh is invested, you will be liable to tax on $16 \times 10/40 =$ Rs. 4 lakh, being the long-term capital gain. Also see Chapter 5, topic 5.

Q.29.   I am an NRI. I have made a long-term capital gain of Rs. 12 lakh on the sale of a plot of land in Faridabad. I do not intend to buy any immovable property in India. Still I wish to get complete exemption from income tax on the long-term capital gains. Is it possible?

Ans.   Yes. Refer to Chapter 5, topic 6.

Q.30.   I and my uncle are partners in a partnership firm in New Delhi. I am now an NRI. We wish to convert the partnership firm into a private limited company and transfer all the assets to that company. Is it possible to get full exemption from income tax?

Ans.   Yes. See Chapter 5, topic 7.

Q.31.   I am an NRI. However, my wife is in India for the education of our children. She is running a Boutique. She wants to convert her business into a private limited company and take me also as a shareholder and a Director. Is it possible to do so without attracting any income tax on the capital gains?

Ans.   Yes. See Chapter 5, topic 8.

Q.32.   I am an NRI. My father is the karta of a Hindu undivided family in New Delhi. We are three brothers. He has made a total partition of the HUF. I have received Rs. 80 lakh worth of immovable property in complete partition of the HUF. Am I liable to any capital gains tax in India.

Ans.   No. See Chapter 5, topic 9(2).

Q.33.   My uncle has made a Will in which he has given me a house property worth Rs. 1.2 crore. He died recently. Am I liable to any capital gains tax in India on the receipt of the immovable property through Will?

Ans.   No. You will be completely exempt from income-tax regarding receipt of the property by Will. See Chapter 5, topic 9(3).

Q.34.   I am an NRI. I was a shareholder in a company which has affected demerger as per provisions of the Income Tax Act. In the Scheme of Demerger I have received certain shares, the market value of which is higher than the value of shares originally bought by me. Will I be liable to any income tax on the gains?

Ans.   No. Such a transaction is completely exempt from income tax. See Chapter 5, topic 9(10).

Q.35.   I am an NRI. I invested Rs. 2 crore in the acquisition of NRI bonds through foreign exchange. I have transferred these bonds outside India to a non-resident and made a gain of Rs. 35 lakh. Am I liable to any income tax in India.

Ans.   No. See Chapter 5, topic 9(12).

Q.36.   I am an NRI. I have lent certain securities to another NRI as per the guidelines issued by the SEBI. Is this transaction considered as a transfer for the purpose of capital gain tax?

Ans.   No. See Chapter 5, topic 9(14).

Q.37.   I am the owner of an agricultural land in India for the last 12 years. For the last four years my father has been carrying on the agricultural operations on this land. If I sell this agricultural land, I can make a profit of Rs. 20 lakh. How can this income be exempt?

Ans.   See Chapter 5, topic 9(15).

Q.38.   I am an NRI. I live in the USA. I have a house property in Ajmer. I made advertisements in the newspaper and incurred Rs. 70,000 in connection with the sale. Finally, I have been able to sell the property at a gain of Rs. 5 lakh. Can I get a deduction of Rs. 70,000 for the purpose of income tax?

Ans.   Yes. Refer to Chapter 5, topic 10.

Q.39.   I am an NRI. I acquired a plot of land, through inheritance in the year 1978. The market value of the said plot as on 1.4.1981 was Rs. 10 lakh. I have disposed of the same in the financial year 2006-2007 for Rs. 40 lakh and thus, made a gain of about Rs. 30 lakh. Am I liable to any income tax on the capital gains?

Ans.   No. The acquisition price of Rs. 10 lakh would be enhanced by the Cost Inflation Index which is 519 for the financial year 2006-2007. Hence, the cost price will be considered as Rs. 51,90,000. As the sale price is less than that, there will not be any income tax payable by you for the A.Y. 2007-2008. Also see Chapter 5, topic 10.

Q.40.   I am an NRI at present. I have been a tenant for the last 15 years in a house property in New Delhi. The landlord wanted me to quit the house and get some compensation for it. I got Rs. 10 lakh for vacating the flat. Will I be liable to income tax on Rs. 10 lakh,

Ans.   Yes. You will be required to pay income-tax on long term capital gains on the surrender of tenancy rights. See Chapter 5, topic 10.

Q.41.   I am an NRI. I have sold certain shares of a private limited company in India at a gain of Rs. 3 lakh and kept the said shares for a period of two years before their sale. These shares were purchased out of my NRO Account. Can I pay the concessional rate of income tax of 10% on the same?

Ans.   No. As the shares are not listed on a stock exchange, you will not be liable to the concessional income tax rate of 10 per cent. See Chapter 5, topic 11.

Q.42.   I got certain shares under ISPO. I have, however, gifted the same to my son. The market value on the date of gift is Rs. 5 lakh. Will he be liable to income tax on an amount of Rs. 5 lakh.

Ans.   Yes. It will be treated as a capital gain liable to income tax. Refer to Chapter 5, topic 13.

Wealth Tax

Q.43.   As an NRI, I own a plot of land of 400 sq.mts. in a posh colony of New Delhi. Its market value is Rs. 20 lakh. Besides, I own jewellery worth Rs. 8 lakh in India. I have no other asset in India. Am I liable to wealth tax?

Ans.   The plot of land is exempt from wealth-tax. As the value of the only other asset in jewellery is below Rs. 15 lakh, you will not be required to pay any wealth tax in India. Also refer to Chapter 6, topic 3.

Q.44.   I am an NRI. I own two residential flats in a posh building at Mumbai. These are let out for the entire year. Am I liable to any wealth tax on the market value of the property, which is about Rs. 2 crore?

Ans. You are not liable to any wealth-tax as the residential property has been let out for a minimum 300 days. Also see Chapter 6, topic 2.

Q.45. As an NRI, I do not own any immovable property excepting one self-occupied house valued at Rs. 2 crores where my children reside for study purposes. I own bank fixed deposits and units in Mutual Funds and also certain deposits in companies was Rs. 70 lakh. Am I liable to any wealth tax in India?

Ans. No. These are all exempt from wealth tax. Refer to Chapter 6, topic 2.

Q.46. As an NRI, I do not own any immovable property in India. However, I own two imported cars valued at Rs. 50 lakh. Will I be liable to wealth tax in India?

Ans. Yes. You will be liable to 1 per cent wealth tax on the net value of Rs. 35 lakhs (Rs. 50 lakh — 15 lakh), being the value of motor cars. Also refer to Chapter 6, para 2.

Q.47. I have immovable property outside India worth Rs. 50 crore. I am an NRI. I have only one self-occupied flat in India. Am I liable to any wealth tax?

Ans. No. See Chapter 6, topic 5.

Foreign Exchange Assets

Q. 48. I am an NRI. I have invested foreign exchange equivalent to Rs. 40 lakh in debentures of a private limited company, on which I get regular interest amounting to Rs. 6 lakh every year. Am I liable to income-tax in India at any special rate or at the normal rate of tax. Am I liable to the income tax at 20% or like resident individuals.

Ans. As the debentures are issued by the Indian company which is a private company, they are not considered as specified assets for Section 115C. Hence, you will be liable to tax at the normal rate like any residential individual and not at a special rate of 20%. Also see Chapter 7, topic 4.

Q.49. I have made deposits with a public limited company in India by remitting foreign exchange in dollars. I am getting Rs. 5 lakh interest every year. What is rate of income tax applicable to me?

Ans.   You will be liable to income tax at the rate of 20% on the investment income from specified assets as per Section 115E. Refer to Chapter 7, topic 5.

Q.50.   My long-term capital gain as an NRI in respect of foreign exchange assets this year would be Rs. 12 lakh. What is the income tax payable by me?

Ans.   You will be required to pay income tax at 10% on the long-term capital gains as per Section 115E. See also Chapter 7, topic 5.

Q.51.   As an NRI, I remitted dollars and invested the same in debentures. My annual interest of these debentures is Rs. 10 lakh. The income tax has been deducted at source by the company on the interest income. As I have no other income in India, am I still liable to file an income tax return in India?

Ans.   No. Refer Chapter 7, topic 7.

Q.52.   As an NRI, I sent US dollars for investment in deposits of a public limited company in India. Now I have come back to India for good. I wish that the sum of Rs. 10 lakh be assessable for the next four years being the term of the deposit at 20% special rate of income tax only. Is it possible? What should I do?

Ans.   Yes. It is possible. As per Section 115H, you should exercise your option to be assessable at the special rate of 20% on the investment income in future as well. See Chapter 7, topic 8.

Q.53.   As an NRI, I made investments in debentures of a public company by remitting dollars from USA. My annual income from interest is Rs. 1,10,000 for F.Y. 2006-07. I am told that I would be liable to income tax at 20% on the entire sum of Rs. 1,10,000. Is there any way to minimise tax?

Ans.   Yes. You should exercise your option not to be governed by the provisions of Chapter XII-A, i.e. the levy of income tax at the special rate of 20% on the entire investment income. Thus, like a normal resident you will be liable to pay income tax only Rs. 1,000 and not Rs. 22,000 at 20% on Rs. 1,10,000. Also refer to Chapter 7, topic 9.

Deductions

Q.54. I wish to open an account in a Post Office for PPF and deposit Rs. 70,000 therein. How much income-tax benefit shall I get from the income tax payable in India for the F.Y. 2007-078.

Ans. For the A.Y. 2008-09 (i.e. for F.Y. 2007-08) as per Section 80C deduction @100% would be available on Rs. 70,000. Also refer to Chapter 8, topic 3.

Q.55. I am a senior citizen aged 72 years. I am an NRI. How much income-tax deduction would be given to me in respect of income-tax payable by me on my Indian income?

Ans. The higher exemption limit for a senior citizen is admissible only to a resident and not for an NRI. Also refer to Chapter 8, topic 3.

Q.56. I am a married lady settled in the USA. However, I have got rental income of Rs. 2,00,000 in India. How much tax benefit shall I get for being a woman?

Ans. You will not be entitled to any special tax deduction for being a woman NRI. The higher exemption for women tax payers is only for resident women tax payers.

Q.57. I have contributed Rs. 2 lakh for the Prime Minister's Relief Fund for the earthquake victims. How much deduction shall I get as an NRI in respect of my total income in India, which is Rs. 6 lakh.

Ans. You will get full 100% deduction in respect of Rs. 2 lakh. See Chapter 8, topic 4.

Q.58. As an NRI, I have one NRO A/c in India from which I get an interest of Rs. 2,50,000 every year. Shall I get complete exemption in respect of the interest?

Ans. For the A.Y. 2007-08 no deduction is permissible from Bank interest. You will have to pay tax on Rs. 2,50,000 as per the slabs. Also refer to Chapter 8, topic 5.

Q.59. What is the tax benefit available for starting and operating an infrastructural facility in India?

Ans. Refer to Chapter 8, topic 6.

Q.60. I propose to develop and maintain an industrial park in India as per Notification of the government. Will I get complete exemption from income tax?

Ans. Yes, for initial five years. Also refer to Chapter 8, topic 7.

Q.61. I come from a District of Rajasthan which has been declared as a very backward District. I propose to set up an industry there. What is the income tax exemption in respect of the profits from the industries set up in that area?

Ans. Refer to Chapter 8, topic 8.

Q.62. As an NRI I sometimes visit India and stay upto 30 days in India. I have taken medical insurance on my life and pay a premium of Rs. 10,000. Will this amount be deductible from taxable income?

Ans. Yes. Refer to chapter 8, topic 10.

Q.63. I am an NRI. I have a physically handicapped child in India on whose medical treatment I spent about Rs. 2 lakh every 6 years. How much tax deduction shall be allowed in computing my taxable income for the same?

Ans. Nil, as this deduction is allowed only to residents. Also refer to Chapter 8, topic 10.

Q.64. I am an NRI. My son is studying in an Engineering College in India. He has taken a loan which would become repayable from the next year, and he will start earning income in India. What deduction would be allowed to him in computing his taxable income?

Ans. Refer to Chapter 8, topic 11.

Q.65. As an NRI, if I export some goods from India to the USA, shall I be eligible to 50% deduction of the export profits for the A.Y. 2002-2003?

Ans. This deduction is allowed only to the residents. Also see Chapter 8, topic 12.

Q.66. I have formed a private limited company in India which is doing export to the USA for the financial year ending 31st March 2007. My export profits are Rs. 30 lakh. How much exemption shall be given to me in respect of the said export profits?

Ans. As per the phasing out policy no tax benefit is not available to you.

Income Tax Return & Assessment

Q.67. I own a house and a telephone in India. Am I required to compulsorily file a return even when I have no taxable income in

India because of some economic criteria, popularly known as 1/6 formula?

Ans.   As an NRI, you are exempt from compulsorily filing of a return as per economic criteria. See Chapter 9, topic 2. Please also note that on and from the A.Y. 2006-07 the requirement of filing return due to fulfilment of economic indicator has been done away with for resident tax payers also.

Q.68.   As an NRI, I have taxable income in India for the financial year ending on 31st March, 2007, relevant to the assessment year 2007-2008. I did not file any return of income. Can the Assessing Officer require me to file an income tax return?

Ans.   Yes. Refer to Chapter 9, topic 3.

Q.69.   The tax payable by me as an NRI in India is much less than the income tax deducted at source. I am eligible to get a refund of Rs. 80,000. What should I do?

Ans.   You should file an income tax return and an application for refund to the concerned Assessing Officer. Refer to Chapter 9, topic 4.

Q.70.   I have filed a return of income for the A.Y. 2007-2008. The Income Tax Officer has served a notice asking me to produce some evidence in support of my income of Rs. 21 lakh in India. Can he do so?

Ans.   Yes. Refer to Chapter 9, topic 6.

Q.71.   As an NRI, my turnover in India from business exceeds Rs. 1 crore. Is it compulsory for me to get the audit of accounts done.

Ans.   Yes. Refer to Chapter 9, topic 6.

Q.72.   I did not appear before the Assessing Officer in response to his notice as I was out of India. As there was no representative of mine in India, the Assessing Officer could not be informed in time. However, he has now made an ex-parte assessment and added Rs. 5 lakh to my total income on estimate. What should I do?

Ans.   You should file an appeal against the Assessing Officer to the CIT (Appeals). Refer to Chapter 9, topic 7.

Q.73.   Taxable income from house rent in India for A.Y. 2007-2008 is Rs. 5 lakh. However, I could not file an income tax return by 31st July 2007. It will be delayed by six months. Shall I be required to pay any penal interest for the delay?

Ans. You have to pay penal interest at the rate of 1% per month on the tax payable on the basis of the return. Also refer to Chapter 9, topic 10.

Q.74. The tax payable by me as an NRI in India in respect of the rental income received by me for my house property at New Delhi would be Rs. 6 lakh. Am I required to pay any advance tax in respect thereof?

Ans. Yes. Refer to Chapter 9, topic 11.

Q.75. The Assessing Officer has levied an extra tax of Rs. 7,000 by making an assessment on me. What should I do?

Ans. You should file an appeal to the CIT (Appeals) within 30 days of the service of the notice or order and pay a minimum filing fee of Rs. 250.

Q.76. For the A.Y. 2005-2006, I lost an appeal before CIT (Appeals). What should I do to get relief on Rs. 2 lakh, the amount of addition sustained by the CIT (Appeals)? The total income computed by the Assessing Officer was Rs. 1 crore.

Ans. You should file an appeal to the Appellate Tribunal within 60 days from the date on which the order of the CIT (Appeals) was communicated to you. You have to pay the maximum filing fee of Rs. 10,000 before preferring an appeal to the Tribunal. Also refer to Chapter 9, topic 12.

Q.77. The Assessing Officer has made a mistake in taking the figure of Rs. 80,000 as my interest on company deposits as against Rs. 8,000 shown by me. What is the remedy?

Ans. You should file an application for rectification. The time limit is 4 years. Refer to Chapter 9, topic 13.

Q.78. I have good income in India which ranges between Rs. 20 lakh to Rs. 30 lakh every year. I am normally staying in the USA. Can I appoint someone as my agent to look after my income tax matters?

Ans. Yes. Refer to Chapter 9, topic 14.

Q.79. In the newspaper I often hear about a tax-payer in India being required to apply for some PAN. As an NRI, I have a taxable income of Rs. 5 lakh per year, am I required to apply for and obtain PAN.

Ans. No. You are exempt from complying with the provisions regarding PAN. See also Chapter 9, topic 15.

Q.80.   I have sold my plot of land valuing Rs. 12 lakh to a buyer of New Delhi. He has requested me to obtain a tax clearance certificate. I have told him that as an NRI I am exempted from doing so. Am I required to obtain a tax clearance certificate by applying in Form No. 34A.

Ans.   Yes. See Chapter 9, topic 16.

Q.81.   As I have jewellery exceeding Rs. 15 lakh, I understand that I am required to file a wealth tax return. Is the procedure of making the wealth tax assessment different from income tax assessment procedure? Please enlighten.

Ans.   Refer to Chapter 9, topic 18.

Gift by NRIs

Q.82.   In the month of August, 1998, I made a gift of US Dollars 1 lakh by means of a bank draft sent from the USA. Am I required to pay any gift tax in this regard.

Ans.   No.

Q.83.   I have made a gift of immovable property situated in the USA to my son who is studying in India. The gift was made on 28.4.1998. The value of the gift was US Dollars 2 lakh. Am I required to pay any gift tax in India because my son was in India.

Ans.   No.

Q.84.   I, as an NRI, gave a gift of Rs. 20 lakh to my school friend out of moneys lying in my Non-resident (External) Account in Mumbai. The gift was made on 8.7.1998 on the occasion of his wedding anniversary. I have been told that I may be required to pay some gift tax.

Ans.   The gift is completely exempt from gift tax.

Q.85.   On 23.11.1997, I made a gift of a foreign exchange asset to my eldest son in India. The value of the gift is US $1.5 lakh. Please enlighten me about the gift tax implications of this gift.

Ans.   This gift was exempt from gift tax. Refer to Chapter 10.

Q.86.   I have made a gift of Rs. 10 lakh out of my NRO Account to my respected father on 28.4.2007. Is there any gift tax implication.

Ans.   It is also fully exempt. Refer to Chapter 10.

FEMA and NRIs

Q.87. Will there be a criminal action on violation of FEMA in the matter of keeping foreign exchange in India against FEMA rules?

Ans. No. Please see Chapter 11, topic 2.

Q.88. I have been in India since my birth. In April, 2007, I am leaving India for employment in the U.S. Will I be considered as a person resident outside India as per FEMA?

Ans. Yes. Please see Chapter 11, topic 3.

Q.89. I propose to leave India in May 2007 to meet my relatives in the USA and to stay for about 250 days with them. My stay in India will be less than 280 days. Will I be considered as an NRI as a person outside India, as per FEMA?

Ans. No. See Chapter 11, topic 3.

Q.90. Though several regulations have been made under FEMA, yet I am an NRI to get any guidance from the Exchange Control Manual in some matters?

Ans. Yes. See Chapter 11, topic 7.

Q.91. I inherited immovable property in India worth Rs. 2 crore from my grandfather two years ago. Last year I left India for taking up a job in U.K. Can I continue to hold the property in India or am I required to do anything under the FEMA?

Ans. You have not to do anything. You can continue to hold the property in India. Refer to Chapter 12, topic 2.

Q.92. I am an NRI. I am a citizen of India. Can I acquire any immovable property in India other than agricultural/plantation property or a farm house without applying to the RBI?

Ans. Yes. Refer to Chapter 12, topic 3.

Q.93. I am a citizen of USA, but I am a person of Indian citizen. Can I buy the property in India?

Ans. Yes. See Chapter 12, topic 4.

Q.94. As an NRI, I want to establish a Branch in New Delhi. For the same, I wish to acquire a flat at Connaught Place. Am I permitted to do so under the FEMA?

Ans. Yes. Refer Chapter 12, topic 5.

Q.95.   As an NRI, I have purchased a property in India last year. This year, I wish to remit the sale proceeds of foreign exchange to the USA. Am I permitted to do so?

Ans.   The sale should take place after three years from the date of acquisition of the property then only the sale proceeds can be permitted in foreign exchange. See Chapter 12, topic 6.

Q.96.   I purchased six flats in New Bombay for about seven years ago. I wish to remit the sale proceeds of one flat sold by me this year back to the USA. Can I do so without the permission of RBI under FEMA.

Ans.   Yes. Refer to Chapter 12, topic 6.

Q.97.   I am a citizen of Nepal. Can I acquire the property in India without the permission of the RBI?

Ans.   No. See Chapter 12, topic 7.

Q.98.   I am a Pakistani citizen. However, I am an NRI as my father was born in India. Can I buy a flat in Ajmer?

Ans.   No. Refer to Chapter 12, topic 7.

Q.99.   As an NRI, I have won 10 lakh rupees in lottery winnings. Can I remit the amount by foreign exchange under the FEMA?

Ans.   No. See Chapter 13, topic 2.

Q.100.   I am an NRI. I want to organise a foreign cultural tour of India to the USA. Can I spend the foreign exchange for the same purpose?

Ans.   As you are a resident of India, the remittance on current account transaction requires the permission of the Ministry of HRD. See Chapter 13, topic 3.

Q.101.   I want to make donation exceeding US $ 5,000 this year to my son studying in America. Can I do so without the permission of the RBI?

Ans.   You have to take the permission of the RBI. Refer to Chapter 13, topic 4 and topic 5.

Q.102.   I am an NRI. I wish to be a partner in a partnership firm doing a chit fund business in Chennai. Am I permitted to do so under FEMA?

Ans.   See Chapter 14, topic 4.

Q.103.   I am an NRI. My brother is doing the business of construction of farm houses in New Delhi. He has invited me to join him as a partner. Am I permitted to do so?

Ans.   No. Refer to Chapter 14, topic 4.

Q.104.   As an NRI, I am interested in making direct investment in certain businesses. Please let me know the regulation in this regard under FEMA.

Ans.   See Chapter 15, topic 3.

Q.105.   I am the Chairman of a firm of Foreign Institutional Investors (FII). What are the rules under FEMA for the Portfolio Investment Scheme. Does the limit of 5% of the paid-up capital of each series of convertible debentures exist under FEMA also?

Ans.   Yes. Refer to Chapter 15, topic 4.

Q.106.   As an NRI, I wish to invest US $ 2 lakh in the purchase of Reliance shares. Am I to seek any permission through the broker in Mumbai. Have I to seek any permission of the RBI under FEMA?

Ans.   No. Refer to Chapter 15, topic 5.

Q.107.   As an NRI, I wish to buy convertible debentures on non-repatriation basis by investing Rs. 20 lakh out of NR (External) Account. Have I to obtain the permission of the RBI?

Ans.   No. Refer to Chapter 15, topic 7.

Q.108.   I am an NRI for the last five years. Can I open a Non-Resident (External) Account and get back the amount in foreign exchange as and when I require.

Ans.   Yes. Refer to Chapter 16, topic 2.

Q.109.   After being an NRI for 20 years, I am returning to India for doing some business in India and with an intention for settling in India permanently. Have I to convert my NRE account?

Ans.   Yes. Your NRE account should be converted to RFC account immediately on your return to India for the purposes of carrying on business in India. Refer to Chapter 16, topic 3.

Q.110.   I am an NRI. I wish to remit $ 1 lakh for deposit in FCNR account in a bank in India. Am I required to seek the permission of the RBI? What is the procedure?

Ans.   Refer to Chapter 16, topic 4.

Q.111.   I received dividend on shares in India and I wish to keep the same in India for spending in India, as and when I come to India. As an NRI can I open any NRO account?

Ans.   Yes. Refer to Chapter 16, topic 5.

Q.112. What are the terms for opening NRNR Deposit account?
Ans.   Refer to Chapter 16, topic 6.

Q.113. Can I, as an NRI, open a NR (Special) Rupee Account in India? What is the procedure to follow?
Ans.   Refer to Chapter 16, topic 7.

Q.114. I am an NRI. My father is the proprietor of a business in New Delhi. Can I make a deposit in his concern on non-repatriation basis?
Ans.   Yes. Refer to Chapter 16, topic 9.

Q.115. As an NRI, I wish to return to India and still maintain my foreign exchange reserves in deposit. Is it possible?
Ans.   Yes. Refer to Chapter 17, topic 2.

Q.116. I earned interest on a RFC account. Now, I have returned to India and become a resident. I stayed abroad for about 20 years. Can I get the income tax exemption on the interest earned by me in the RFC account?
Ans.   Yes. Refer to Chapter 17, topic 3.

Q.117. As an NRI, I stayed abroad for only ten months. Can I open RFC account?
Ans.   No. Refer to Chapter 17, topic 3.

Q.118. I am having hundred per cent export-oriented units in India. I want to open a Foreign Exchange Reserve account for investment abroad. Is it possible to do so? What are the formalities?
Ans.   You can open an EEFC account in India. Refer to Chapter 17, topic 4.

Q.119. I am a returning NRI. I wish to make a direct investment outside India out of my RFC account. Is it possible to do so?
Ans.   Yes. Refer to Chapter 17, topic 5.

Q.120. As an NRI, I inherited immovable property in the USA from my uncle who was also an NRI. Can I hold the property outside India without the RBI's permission under FEMA.
Ans.   Yes. Refer to Chapter 18, topic 2.

Q.121. As an NRI, I am interested in making investment in a proprietary concern in India. What are the formalities to be observed in this connection under FEMA?
Ans.   Refer to Chapter 18, topic 3.

Q.122. I am interested in borrowing money in foreign exchange. What are the limits of such borrowings and what are the formalities to be observed? Please let me know.

Ans.   Refer to Chapter 18, topic 4.

Q.123. As an NRI, can I lend money in rupees in India?

Ans.   Yes. Refer to Chapter 18, topic 5.

Q.124. What are the FEMA Regulations regarding Guarantees, Insurance, and other matters, which I, as an NRI, should know?

Ans.   Refer to Chapter 18, topics 6–14.

PERSONAL
Investment
A N D   T A X   P L A N N I N G

Dear Investor,

How to invest your money most profitably — and lower your taxes

"The secret is to first learn, then invest, then go on learning," according to Merril Lynch, global leaders in investment services.

The books featured on the next 7 pages cover the entire gamut of investment, personal finance, and tax planning, packed with expert know-how and guidance both for experienced investors and comparative beginners to investing. Covering all types of investment options and hundreds of tried and tested tax-saving ideas, these books will help you:

▶ Invest your money most profitably; and

▶ Make dramatic tax savings.

Written by top Indian and international experts, hundreds of thousands of satisfied investors have endorsed the value of these books.

Reader Privilege Offer: Save 10% rightaway!

When you order for the books of the value of Rs. 395/- and above you are entitled to a 10% saving on the prices of the books you order;

Act Today. . .
A reply-paid *Reader Privilege Voucher* is included in this book for your ordering convenience. Or, you can send us your order by letter, fax or e-mail. Ordering information is given on page 8 of this booklet.

Yours sincerely,

Kapil Malhotra
Director

Investing for Beginners

Kathy Kristof

This book is simple. It's straightforward. It skilfully guides you step-by-step to investment success. Highlights: ■ Investment Risks and Rewards ■ Your Starting Point ■ How to pick stocks ■ Investing in Bonds ■ Mutual Funds Primer.

Order No. 482-1
Price: Rs. 170/-

"Smart, sensible advice . . . a road map to financial success without gimmicks or secret formulas."
Los Angeles Times, USA

How to Manage Your Investment Risks & Returns

An Essential Self-teaching Guide for Every Investor

David L. Scott

Order No. 394-9
Price: Rs. 145/-

The secret of successful investing lies rather in understanding and controlling the risk involved in any investment. Step-by-step this book shows you how to control your investment risks.

"An object lesson." The Economic Times

INVESTMENT OPTIONS

Profitable investment in shares : *A Beginner's Guide*

S. S. Grewal & Navjot Grewal

This hugely popular book tells you the basic principles and guidelines of profitable investment in shares. It also highlights the basic rules to

Order No. 573-9
Price: Rs. 125/-

follow in order to ensure reasonable safety of your capital. And it does all this in simple, clear language without resorting to jargon or technicalities. So, if are you one of those who wants to invest in shares but doesn't know quite how to go about it, then you can't do much better than starting with this book.

"Positively rewarding." Financial Express

The Basics of Investing

Gerald Krefetz

The rapidly growing number of investment avenues often lead to confusion. In this book, an investment expert offers you the must-know principles, expert guidance and sensible solutions to invest your money profitably.

Order No. 446-5
Price: Rs. 170/-

The Basics of Stocks

Gerald Krefetz

You probably need to invest in shares to achieve long-term capital appreciation. What you also need to do is to do it right. In simple, easy-to-follow steps, a Wall Street expert offers you solutions for making the most out of investing in shares.

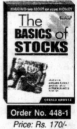

Order No. 448-1
Price: Rs. 170/-

The Basics of Bonds

Profitable Fixed-Income Investing

Gerald Krefetz

The lure: bonds and other fixed income investment avenues offer relatively greater safety of capital with predictable returns.

Order No. 447-3
Price: Rs. 170/-

This book by a U.S. investment expert will assist you in making intelligent decisions about your fixed-income investing.

The Basics of Speculating

How to Speculate Most Profitably with Your Hard-Earned Money

Gerald Krefetz

This book tackles in detail the most popular financial instruments used for speculation: stocks, bonds, options, futures, commodities, precious metals and foreign exchange, etc.,

Order No. 449-X
Price: Rs. 170/-

Personal Investment & Tax Planning Yearbook (A.Y. 2008-09)

How to Invest Your Money Most Profitably This Year

N. J. Yasaswy

Personal Investment & Tax Planning Yearbook
Financial Year 2008-2009
Yasaswy

Order No. 698-0
Price: Rs. 235/-

Are your savings invested profitably enough to buy you a house, provide the best higher education for your children, take you on a vacation abroad or ensure a failsafe retirement income? Whether it is Rs 10,000 you want to invest or Rs 10 lakh, *Personal Investment & Tax Planning Yearbook* shows you the most profitable ways to do so, combining the best investment options and the latest tax incentives offered in the 2006-2007 budget.

WHERE TO INVEST YOUR MONEY THIS YEAR: ■ The investment scene and Budget impact ■ The 50 best equity shares for aggressive investors ■ The 50 best stocks for conservative investors ■ Corporate debentures and public sector bonds ■ Safe company deposits ■ Where not to invest ■ Performance analysis and long-term outlook of mutual funds ■ *Also*, 10 readymade investment portfolios for you to pick from.

HOW TO SAVE TAXES THIS YEAR ■ Sensible, practical guidance on tax planning, including income tax and wealth tax ■ How to lower your tax rates through long-term capital gains from growth shares ■ How to achieve a zero-tax status ■ Tax planning for your whole family ■ Tax deduction, tax-exempt incomes and other tax benefits ■ Your tax calendar for the year ■ *Plus,* how much investment risk you should take.

"Annual ready-reckoner for the investor." *The Hindu*

MUTUAL FUNDS

Indian Mutual Funds Handbook: *A Guide for Industry Professionals and Intelligent Investors*

Sundar Sankaran

Order No. 683-2
Price: Rs. 395/-

This comprehensive handbook by an expert lays out the working of Indian mutual funds, their operational and regulatory mechanisms, the advantages and limitations of investing in them along with suitable approaches to personal financial planning. The author's experience of handling hundreds of training programmes ensures an engaging and easy to understand approach to mastering the subject.

"I recommend this book to everyone who wants to make informed investment decisions"
Shekhar Sathe, Kotak Mahindra

"The best book for understanding (Indian) mutual funds"
M. Subramanian CEO India, Barclays Bank, plc.

"If you think you know everything about mutual funds, read the book to find out how much you don't know!"
Prof. G. Sethu, Dean, UTI Institute of Capital Markets

The New Commonsense Guide to Mutual Funds

Mary Rowland

Order No. 479-1
Price: Rs. 225/-

In this top-selling book, one of America's pre-eminent financial journalists, cuts through the hype and confusion surrounding mutual funds and tells you exactly what you need to know.

"Remarkable!" *John C. Bogle*

The Winning Portfolio

How to choose the best mutual funds

Paul B. Farrell

Order No. 481-3
Price: Rs. 145/-

Farrell's strategy is easy-to-follow and will help diversify your portfolio while shielding your investment from market downturns.

"An easy-to-follow roadmap for maximizing your mutual funds profits. . . both rational and intuitive" *Brian Murray*

Intelligent Stock Market Investing
How to Win the Dalal Street Game

N.J. Yasaswy

Framework for intelligent investing. "Packs a lot of substance." *Business India*

No. 695-6 | Rs. 280/-

Stock Market Logic
A Sophisticated Approach to Profits on Wall Street

Norman G. Fosback

Hundreds of sophisticated investment techniques. "Classic." *Joseph Granville.*

No. 440-6 | Rs. 235/-

Fundamental Analysis for Investors

Raghu Palat

"A masterly introduction to fundamental analysis." *Times of India*

No. 569-0 | Rs. 190/-

Balance Sheets
Contents, Analysis & Interpretation

Hemant R. Dani

How to interpret and analyse financial statements . . . of great value for investors

No. 476-7 | Rs. 190/-

The Indian Securities Market
BEST SELLER!
A Guide for Foreign & Domestic Investors

Tadashi Endo

"The best book on India's securities industry. . ."
Business India
"Brilliant." *Business Standard*

No. 386-8 | Rs. 395/-

The Stock Market Dictionary
Guide to Dalal Street Money-Talk
BEST SELLER!

Praveen N. Shroff

Nearly, 2,000 stock market terms clearly defined and explained. **"Well worth possessing."** *Financial Express*

No. 436-8 | Rs. 190/-

The Tough-Minded Investor: Pistolese

This book will help you understand how emotional decision making may be hurting your chances for success. It outlines long-term strategies to help you avoid the emotional stress of sharp, short-term price fluctuations.

No. 219-5 | Rs. 125/-

Value Averaging
Systematic investment techniques for fail-safe stock market returns

Michael E. Edleson

How value averaging helps you automatically buy low and sell high — without market timing and stock-picking techniques.

No. 228-4 | Rs. 125/-

It's When You Sell That Counts
It's Not *What Stocks You Buy. . .*

Donald L. Cassidy

You haven't made your profits until you have the money in hand — and that doesn't happen until you sell your shares.

"Just as Peter Lynch stripped away the mystique of buying stocks... Don Cassidy successfully answers the question, 'When do I sell?'" *R. Jerry Falkner, CFA*

"Should be required reading for all investors."
Phoenix Balance Fund, USA

No. 561-5 | Rs. 235/-

100 World-Famous Stock Market Techniques: Richard J. Maturi
BEST SELLER!

One-of-a-kind, handy reference that provides concise descriptions of one hundred of the most important stock market investment methods used worldwide. . . describes how each method works — and how and when it can be used to best advantage.

"The best book of its kind." *Business Standard*

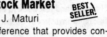

No. 562-3 | Rs. 190/-

Timing the Market: How to Profit in Bull & Bear Markets with Technical Analysis
Curtis M. Arnold

"The Bible of Technical Analysis."
MBH Commodity Advisors, USA

"Excellent." *Money, USA*   No. 662-X   *Rs. 235/-*

Elliot Wave Explained
Robert C. Beckman

The clearest and easiest-to-understand discussion of Elliot Wave Theory ever published.
No. 532-1   *Rs. 395/-*

The Technical Analysis Course
A Winning Program for Investors & Traders
Thomas A. Meyers

When, where and how to employ the different techniques and tools of technical analysis.
Plus: lessons and quizzes.   No. 489-9   *Rs. 325/-*

Candlestick Charting Explained
Timeless Techniques for Trading Stocks and Futures
Gregory L. Morris   BEST SELLER!

"Arguably the best book on candles, tying them together, for the first time, with traditional technical analysis." *Technical Trends, USA*   No. 240-3   *Rs. 395/-*

Martin Pring on Market Momentum   BEST SELLER!
Martin J. Pring

"There's gold in these pages — the definitive guide to momentum." *Traders Press, USA*   No. 570-4   *Rs. 395/-*

Technical Analysis for Futures Traders
Darrel R. Jobman

A Comprehensive Guide to Analytical Methods, Trading Systems and Technical Indicators.   No. 577-1   *Rs. 495/-*

The Technical Analysis of Stocks, Options & Futures
William F. Eng

"Encyclopedic in scope . . . should be in every trader's library." *Chicago Board of Trade.*   No. 531-3   *Rs. 495/-*

Stock Market Probability
Joseph E. Murphy

"Brilliant... refines your decision-making"
Business Standard   No. 200-4   *Rs. 280/-*

Using Technical Analysis: The Basics
Cliford Pistolese

"Enables investors to take profitable decisions."
Business India   No. 391-4   *Rs. 190/-*

International Encyclopedia of Technical Analysis
Joel G. Seigel, Jae K. Shim, Anique Qureshi, Jeffrey Brauchier

A-to-Z of Technical Analysis for trading stocks, derivatives and Commodities   No. 648-4   *Rs. 495/-*

Technical Analysis from A-to-Z   BEST SELLER!
Steven B. Achelis

"All aspects of technical analysis in one easily digestible book . . . a must for investors."
Steven Nison   No. 312-4   *Rs. 395/-*

Technical Analysis of Stock Trends, 8th Ed.
Robert Edwards & John Magee

"Classic" reference on analyzing trends; packed with time-tested techniques   No. 663-8   *Rs. 595/-*

The Psychology of Technical Analysis   BEST SELLER!
Tony Plummer

"Will entertain and intrigue the keen investors."
Financial Times, London   No. 492-9   *Rs. 395/-*

How to Make Money Trading Derivatives: *An Insider's Guide (2nd Edition)*
Ashwani Gujral

This is a pioneering book on trading derivatives in the Indian market.

The book focuses on: ■ Technical tools for traders ■ Profitable day trading ■ Cash and futures arbitrage to make profits from idle cash ■ Futures trading strategies ■ Option trading strategies ■ The high returns ■ Covered call writing strategies ■ Trading during special events, such as elections, company results.

"Gujral has cemented himself as a pioneer in this field" *James Holter, Editor, Futures Magazine, USA.*

Order No. 682-3
Price: Rs. 395/-

Order No. 691-3
Price: Rs. 280/-

Futures and Options
Introduction to Equity Derivatives
R. Mahajan

How derivatives work and how you can benefit from them to protect your stock market investment is the thrust of this book.

The book lays particular emphasis on stock index futures — the first risk-proofing tool available to the Indian investor. The author explains both the underlying concepts and procedures in a straightforward manner. Assuming no prior knowledge, both the beginners and market operators will find this easy-to-understand book to get started in futures and options.

"An excellent introduction to derivatives"
Anand Rathi, President, The Stock Exchange, Mumbai

Order No. 555-0
Price: Rs. 395/-

New Insights on Writing Covered Call Options
The Powerful Technique that Enhances Return and Lowers Risk in Stock Investing
Richard Lehman and Lawrence G. McMillan

In this pioneering, easy-to-understand book, leading options experts, give a complete guide to covered call writing and the increased control and lowered risk it affords. They detail the basics and beyond, from the mechanics of implementation to developing strategies that are best suited to your investment goals.

"This book makes a great case for basic reading and writing — reading stock charts and writing covered calls" *John Murphy*

"This was a definite eye-opener and one of the soundest approaches to stock investing I've seen. It makes you wonder what else Wall Street has been keeping from us" *Brian R. Workman*

Order No.520-8
Price: Rs. 395/-

Profit in the Futures Markets!
Insights and Strategies for Futures and Futures Options Trading
Jake Bernstein

Filled with practical tools and techniques for understanding and prospering in the world of futures trading, *Profit in the Futures Markets!* shows how to use such information to your best advantage.

"One of best books I've ever seen on the futures markets" *Rick Bensignor, Chief Technical Strategist, Morgan Stanley*

"Jake Bernstein is one of the best at putting together the emotions and mechanics of trading"
Futures Magazine, USA

Order No. 331-0
Price: Rs. 325/-

Dictionary of Futures and Options
Over 1,500 Terms Defined and Explained
Alan Webber

The *Dictionary of Futures and Options* is a comprehensive reference source of essential information for any investor involved in futures and options. Both the complete beginner and the seasoned professional will find this book invaluable. It contains all the basic terminology.

"Reference book on futures and options" *The Hindu*

How to Save Income Tax through Tax Planning

Practical and time-tested methods for saving income tax: R. N. Lakhotia & Subhash Lakhotia
This book provides expert guidance about the different methods of tax planning.

"Packed with hundreds of ready-to-use tax saving ideas." *The Hindu*
No. 665-4 *Rs. 190/-*

Tax Planning for NRIs

R. N. Lakhotia

Full of practical examples, this book describes how proper tax planning can protect the foreign income of NRIs from being taxed in India.

"No NRI can afford to navigate the Indian tax ocean without this book." *President, American Association of NRIs*
No. 672-7 *Rs. 225/-*

Income Tax Guide

Expert Guidance on Computation of Tax and Trouble-Free Assessments

R. N. Lakhotia

Here is must-know expert guidance on: ■ How to compute your taxable income from different sources: ■ Which incomes are taxed, and which are not ■ Assessment and appeals procedure.
No. 673-5 *Rs. 145/-*

Tax Guru — 51 Income Tax Tips for Investors

Subhash Lakhotia

Tapping "Invisible" Funds ■ Avoid Clubbing of Wife's Income ■ Money Making Ideas in Real Estate ■ Joint Bank Account ■ **Plus much more. . .**
No. 669-7 *Rs. 145/-*

Tax Doctor — 51 Tips for Saving Income Tax

Subhash Lakhotia

How not to Pay any Income Tax at all ■ Let Your Adult Children be Your Tax Saver Too ■ Plus much more. . . .
No. 668-9 *Rs. 145/-*

Taxpayer to Taxsaver

A. N. Shanbhag

A best-selling author's expert guidance on how to be a taxsaver instead of a taxpayer — solutions that work.
No. 697-2 *Rs. 235/-*

How to Save Tax on Your Salary & Perquisites: R.N. Lakhotia

Your A to Z salary and perquisite planner for lower taxes and higher take-home pay.

"With these tips a salaried taxpayer can halve his tax obligation, and in some cases avoid it totally" *The Tribune*
No. 677-8 *Rs. 145/-*

How to Save Tax on Capital Gains

R. N. Lakhotia

This book shows how you can save tax on your capital gains through an analysis of various relevant tax provisions.
No. 676-X *Rs. 190/-*

Tax-Free Incomes & Investments

R.N. Lakhotia

India's taxation expert briefs you on more than 100 items of tax-free incomes and investments which result in tax-free income.
No. 674-3 *Rs. 190/-*

रुपया कहां इन्वैस्ट करें

राम निवास लखोटिया एवं सुभाष लखोटिया
इस पुस्तक में विभिन्न निवेशों की जानकारी, अलग-अलग शीर्षक देकर दी गई है तथा साथ ही यह भी बताया गया है कि प्रत्येक निवेश पर कितना और कैसे कर बचाया जा सकता है।
No. 694-8 *Rs. 125/-*

इन्कम टैक्स कैसे बचाएं

राम निवास लखोटिया
इस पुस्तक में सुप्रसिद्ध कर-विशेषज्ञ रामनिवास लखोटिया ने कर-नियोजन के कई महत्वपूर्ण और कानूनी तरीकों के बारे में वह जानकारी प्रस्तुत की है कि कर कैसे बचाया जा सकता है।
No. 696-4 *Rs. 145/-*

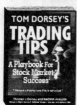

Tom Dorsey's Trading Tips

A Playbook for Stock Market Success

Thomas J. Dorsey and the DWA Analysts

This book lays down a simple but effective and disciplined trading methodology for stock market success.

"Reading Dorsey's recipes is a must." *Frank Capiello*

"A must-read for both the individual investor and the investment advisor."

Gino Toretta, Prudential Securities, Inc, USA

Stock Market Trading Rules: *Fifty Golden Strategies*

BEST SELLER!

William F. Eng

Seasoned investor William F. Eng, streamlines fifty market trading rules, each a strategic gem, showing you how to survive and succeed in the marketplace.

"A great collection of trading rules, and how to apply them to varying market conditions."

CompuTrac, Inc., USA.

Swing Trading: *A Guide to Profitable Short-term Investing*

Marc Rivalland

This book is packed with expert guidance on a disciplined approach to profitable short-term trading — and one by which you can make money both during the market's upswings and downswings.

"Marc Rivalland offers amazing new insight, clarity and refinement to Gann swing charts" *Ashwani Gujral, Author of the bestseller book* How to Make Money Trading Derivatives

Market Masters

How Successful Traders Think, Trade and Invest — & How You can Too!

Jake Bernstein

- Play your own game
- Don't expect immediate results.
- Do your homework.
- Don't force trades. These are just a few of the

dozens of winning tips you'll find in *Market Masters*.

"Ranks among the greatest trading books ever"
Commodities Educational Institute, U.S.A.